The Arduous Path of Post-Soviet Theological Education

Mark R. Elliott

First Fruits Press
Wilmore, Kentucky
c2020

Elliott, Mark R., 1947-
   The arduous path of Post-Soviet theological education / Mark R. Elliott. – Wilmore, Kentucky : First Fruits Press, ©2020.

   202 pages ; cm

   Includes bibliographical references.
   ISBN 9781648170034 (Paperback)
   ISBN 9781648170058 (Mobi)
   ISBN 9781648170041 (uPDF)
   OCLC 1183397078

   1. Christian education--Former Soviet republics. 2. Theology--Study and teaching--Former Soviet republics. 3. Church and state--Former Soviet republics. 4. Theological seminaries--Former Soviet republics 5. Former Soviet republics--Religion--21st century. I. Title.

BL980.S65 P67 2020   322/.1/0947

First Fruits Press
The Academic Open Press of Asbury Theological Seminary
204 N. Lexington Ave., Wilmore, KY 40390
859-858-2236
first.fruits@asburyseminary.edu
asbury.to/firstfruits

DEDICATION

For Darlene, a soulmate and treasure beyond measure through fifty years of marriage, and counting

WORD OF APPRECIATION

The author wishes to express his appreciation to Robert Danielson of First Fruits Press for his assistance with editing and publication.

Table of Contents

Foreword (Walter Sawatsky) i

Introduction 1

Section 1: Opening Doors

    Chapter 1: Protestant Theological Education in the Former Soviet Union: A Summary (1993) 5

    Chapter 2: Increasing Options for Theological Training in East Central Europe and Soviet Successor States (1993) . 9

    Chapter 3: Protestant Theological Education in the Former Soviet Union, 1924-1993 (1994) 13

Section 2: Establishing a Solid Foundation

    Chapter 4: After Communism: The Mixed Blessing of Western Assistance (1995) 35

    Chapter 5: Pastoral Training Under Fire: A Review of Wayne Kenney, " 'A Conspiracy of Learning': Self-Directed Learning Among Protestant Russian Clergy Before 1987" (1997) 47

    Chapter 6: Recent Research on Evangelical Theological Education in Post-Soviet Societies (1999) . . . 51

Section 3: Emerging Concerns

    Chapter 7: Post-Soviet Protestant Theological Education: Come of Age? (1999) 83

    Chapter 8: Globalization in Theological Education: A Mixed Blessing (2004) 89

Section 4: Future Promise and Warnings

    Chapter 9: The Current Crisis in Protestant Theological Education in the Former Soviet Union (2010) . . . 105

    Chapter 10: Lessons from the Long-Shot Bid to Bring Christian Liberal-Arts Education to Russia (2020) . 143

    Chapter 11: Increasing State Restrictions on Russian Protestant Seminaries (2020) 147

Foreword

Walter Sawatsky

When Mark Elliott and I began our scholarly work on the USSR & Eastern Europe in the 1970s, World War II and the Cold War were the events that our teachers remembered. The reassurance we got in the West was that the Soviet Union was not our friend and its system of oppression and threats would never change. But as scholars of the Soviet Union, in particular of its religious developments, we regularly obtained information about what was changing, the emergence of a dissident movement, and the reality that many intellectuals were seeking for something spiritual.

By 1975 it was clear that the Soviet Union was into a steady economic decline, still denying its many social problems due to alcoholism, drug addiction, and a high divorce rate. Then from the mid-1980s Gorbachev's new policies of *glasnost* (new openness) and *perestroika* (restructuring) began pointing in a new direction. Finally in 1988 the authorities allowed a public celebration of a millennium of Christian presence - the baptism of Rus in 988. With it came a dramatic explosion of religious practice. Everyone wanted to see that Bible that had been so long banned, and soon mobile lending libraries for religious books were everywhere in the cities. Pastors and priests were fighting fatigue because so many people were asking them to tell them about God. By now more than 30 years have passed since the "great transformation" (*die Wende* in German), since that movie, "Repentance," with its unforgettable final line, "What use is a road if it does not lead to a church?"

Walter Sawatsky, Ph.D., is professor emeritus of the Anabaptist Mennonite Biblical Seminary, Elkhart, Indiana, author of Soviet Evangelicals Since World War II, and Senior Researcher at the International Baptist Theological Seminary Centre (Amsterdam).

The great shortage was that all the Christian confessions were desperate to find leaders for the churches who in turn needed to be theologically trained. That is the story Mark Elliott tells here with statistics that nearly stagger the mind, with young and old desperate to learn, new converts joining congregations, and church members and leaders needing to adapt to new conditions. So the drastic changes that are the substance of Elliott's essays on theological education are in no way boring. For many readers there will likely be surprises many times over.

Elliott's reporting is organized chronologically. It begins with his 1993 essay on "Increasing Options for Theological Training," including a near explosion of 40 evangelical Bible schools and seminaries, whereas his 1999 overview of "Recent Research" spoke of several hundred such schools and the business of getting to work on some common standards with the help of an accrediting association. But already the quality of students had changed. The first cohort had been experienced pastors and church activists needing seminary-quality training. However, by 1999 the students were largely inexperienced youth, uncertain even of their calling, and too often too sure of what they would teach the people. For example, graduates, influenced by Western, mostly Reformed, visiting professors, were trying to set believers straight about true Calvinist doctrine, whereas the people and older leaders knew a long tradition of an Arminian theology.

By 2004 "Globalization in Theological Education" was proving to be a decidedly "Mixed Blessing." Those foreign faculty who had suddenly appeared, teaching what they knew through a translator, did not recognize how culturally American was their content and style. The "mixed blessing" for the post-Soviet world spelled an initial, massive financial outlay from abroad, followed by a step-by-step reduction of outside support, while students and teachers in the post-Soviet context had learned to depend on such help.

By 2010, it was common to speak of "The Current Crisis in Protestant Theological Education." Elliott presents in clear steps what had changed because of major challenges, including a church-school divide, with the churches viewing the training as "too academic" and "not practical enough." In addition to the failure of foreign teachers to notice and grasp local culture, church leaders were at first so fixated on evangelism and mission that they too seldom connected their efforts with the schools. Likewise, conflicts were emerging as competing denominations proliferated.

Especially difficult was the necessary reworking of theological curricula to fit the context. The need was to add more instruction in counseling and courses on ways to address contemporary issues such as "abortion, divorce, multiple marriages, homosexuality, and women's ministry." Toivo Pilli, now heading a seminary in Estonia and leading graduate studies for the International Baptist Theological Seminary Centre (recently relocated from Prague to Amsterdam) spoke of teaching as a "prophetic task," not only to assist church workers, but also to lead with ideas for "the church to fulfill its mission to society."

Finally comes a very current chapter (2020) addressing "Increasing State Restrictions on Russian Prostestant Seminaries." Ukraine has been spared so far from what follows. Many of us have been watching the steady rise of state controls on religious activity in most of the Central Asian countries, not really to protect an Islamic population, since their theologians are being tortured and imprisoned. In Russia, not only Jehovah's Witnesses, banned outright, but many more-traditional Protestant activists are increasingly facing fines and arrests. The Putin government's anti-Western propaganda has now reached the level that essentially all non-Orthodox institutions are getting minority-status treatment, with local officials often ahead of federal policy in threatening minority traditions.

That appears to be the context to account for the specific list of restrictions Mark Elliott points to, where the precarious existence of all those Protestant/Evangelical schools is nearing its end. Here is the most detailed and judicious assessment of the present moment. We are reminded of the persistence by so many courageous church leaders back in the late 1920s, who went from leading Bible schools to disappearing in the camps of the Gulag. That may not be the outcome this time, but the courage to teach and the creativity to find alternative ways to train, mentor, and teach are the sources of hope Mark points to. So, unless one is already paying close attention, one will surely learn much here. This anthology may well become an opportunity for an exercise in prayer, knowing that God reigns, praying for leaders and students to find the cracks in the doors that seem to be closing.

Introduction
Mark R. Elliott

In February 1993 I assisted Peter and Anita Deyneka (Peter Deyneka Russian Ministries) and Charley Spicer and Jack Graves (Overseas Council for Theological Education) in organizing a meeting of 38 Russian and Ukrainian theological educators at Dom Turista Hotel in Moscow to discuss the needs of their 22 new pastoral training programs in the former Soviet Union. I will never forget the eagerness, energy, and excitement of these administrators and faculty of new Protestant schools--and this in the capital of a now defunct regime that for 72 years had been militant in its advocacy for atheism.

The needs reported in this one-day gathering were overwhelming: no facilities, no libraries, no trained indigenous faculty, and no textbooks. Nevertheless, there was a palpable dynamism in that hotel ballroom that would not brook surrender before the absolutely daunting agenda of resurrecting Protestant pastoral training, training that had completely ceased to exist as of 1929, 64 years prior. Above all, the heart cry was for textbooks. That was the seedbed for what became the Bible Pulpit Series that provided absolutely essential classroom texts funded primarily by the Maclellan Foundation (TN).

I wrote up the story of these beginnings in my first three pieces on theological education published in my *East-West Church & Ministry Report* (1993), in the Billy Graham Center *CenterLine* (1993), and in the *International Bulletin of Missionary Research* (1994). These articles were followed by my concerns regarding an overly western approach to pastoral training (*The Asbury Theological Journal*, 1995) and my summaries and critiques of three doctoral dissertations on theological education in the region (*EWC&M Report*, 1997 and 1999, and *Religion in Eastern Europe*, 1999). Also in 1999 I reported on both impressive strides forward and words of caution in "Post-Soviet Protestant Theological Education: Come of Age?" (*The Asbury Theological Journal*).

In 2004 I reported on my growing anxiety over the mixed blessing of globalization in theological education, parsing its negative consequences for Eurasia and well beyond (*Christian Education Journal*), followed by a rather detailed assessment of the ramifications of a growing enrollment crisis in Eurasian Protestant theological education (*Religion in Eastern Europe*, 2010).

While my 2020 essay on lessons learned from the birth and demise of Moscow's Russian-American Christian University does not treat theological education *per se*, lessons learned from that experiment directly relate to the current challenges facing post-Soviet pastoral training programs (*Christianity Today*). Finally, most recently I have laid out what I consider could potentially be a lethal Russian state assault on Protestant seminaries. Because of the threat I see posed here, I have given more time and effort to this article than to any I have ever written on the subject of Protestant theological education. I see it as a labor of love on behalf of schools that, in my opinion, are on the verge of extinction, short of a providential reversal of fortune (*Religion in Eastern Europe*, 2020).

How did this focus on theological education come about? It all started in the early 1990s when Charley Spicer of Overseas Council (OC) recruited me to participate in site visits to some new, would-be Protestant seminaries in Russia. With Charley Spicer, Jack Graves, and Manfried Kohl, I vividly recall my first meeting with an impressively earnest Peter Penner in rented facilities of what would become St. Petersburg Christian University. Charley later gave me the opportunity to give lectures on Russian church history and missions to OC donors on a memorable Volga boat cruise. In the end, one article led to another as opportunities and crises poured over—and continue to pour over-beleaguered Protestant theological education in the former Soviet Union. May its cause prevail for the sake of the Kingdom in spite of mounting worldly odds against it.

Section I
Opening Doors

Chapter 1

Protestant Theological Education in the Former Soviet Union: A Summary (1993)

For many decades, the only seminary substitute available for would-be evangelical pastors in the former Soviet Union was informal, trial-and-error pulpit practice and pastoral apprenticeship under a senior presbyter. Little can be said on the subject of formal Protestant theological education for most of the Soviet era because, for almost the entire existence of the USSR, it simply did not exist. For part of the 1920s, Evangelical Christians, Baptists, and Adventists operated four Bible schools, while Lutherans in the 1970s and 80s maintained a small theological institute in Tallinn, Estonia. A mere handful of pastors studied abroad from the late 1950s to 1976.

In 1968, the Kremlin gave permission to the All Union Council of Evangelical Christians-Baptists (AUCECB) to launch a correspondence program. By 1979, 272 pastors had completed the eight available courses. Nevertheless, this modest state concession could not even begin to satisfy thousands of pastors' needs for a better understanding of the Bible and evangelical faith. Then came *glasnost*.

In 1990, the pent-up frustrations of evangelicals who endured many decades of persecution, repression, and discrimination exploded in a frenzy of activity leading to the founding of some forty-five programs of theological education between 1990 and 1992.[1] Today, nineteen Protestant residential Bible schools and seminaries report 1587 students currently enrolled in

---

Reprinted with permission from Wheaton College's Billy Graham Center *CenterLine*, Summer 1993, pp. 1-2.

programs of at least one year in length. The eight largest institutions have 100 to 220 students each, while the next eleven in size enroll 18 to 75 students each. As for denominational affiliation, the new schools include 535 Pentecostal and 530 Baptist students and lesser numbers of Lutherans, Adventists, Mennonites, and Methodists. With few exceptions these schools lack texts, libraries, permanent faculties, and permanent facilities. But they possess staff with exceptional dedication and infectious enthusiasm and students who are extraordinarily eager to learn.

To help address these needs, the Billy Graham Center's Institute for East-West Christian Studies, the Overseas Council for Theological Education and Missions, and Peter Deyneka Russian Ministries sponsored a conference in Moscow in February 1993 attended by 38 Russians and Ukrainians representing 22 new Protestant Bible schools and seminaries.

The most critical needs quickly became apparent. No comprehensive master list exists for Christian titles available in Russian and Ukrainian. No clearinghouse exists to provide coordination for translations in progress. (The resulting waste is illustrated by the fact that two schools reported they had both recently completed translations of the same Old Testament survey.) Available copies in translation cannot begin to service present needs.

Conference representatives emphasized their concerns for 1) an organization to facilitate ongoing sharing of information and coordination; 2) permanent facilities; 3) financial support; 4) the establishment of seminary accreditation standards. Delegates hoped for help from abroad, but through a process of East-West interaction, rather than western dictation.

A number of projections would seem reasonably safe to make, even considering the volatile politics and economies of Soviet successor states.

1. In all probability, correspondence programs serving several thousand pastors will continue, especially if economic conditions continue to deteriorate.

2. Continuing political decentralization and growing nationalism will make it increasingly difficult for individual seminaries to draw students from other republics. Crossing borders may grow more difficult.

3. The need for more Christian literature in Ukrainian will increase. Even if 21 percent of Ukraine's population is Russian, and even if a majority of students there can study in Russian, will they want to? Should they have to?

4. Assistance from abroad will prove vital in the development of residential programs, including libraries, literature, faculty, and buildings.

5. Generational tensions in church leadership seem likely with better educated younger pastors and laypeople seeing church life differently from the older leaders and laity who outlived the state assault on religion without benefit of education.

6. Finally, nondenominational schools (enrollment of 366 at present) are likely to grow in importance as western and indigenous parachurch groups plant more and more churches that are neither Baptist nor Pentecostal, *per se*.

Much can be said in a positive manner about the vision and energy of new theological educators in the East, and for the willingness of an array of western evangelical agencies to assist. At the same time, however, sober reflection would suggest that too many institutions have been founded without sufficient consideration for the advisability of collaborative efforts in expensive and labor-intensive areas such as faculty, texts, and library development.

Seminaries in Soviet successor states should consider carefully western models and money and what these entail. Western involvement could sap vitality, foster dependency, and repeat a damaging Third World-First World theological brain drain if assistance is not carefully coordinated.

The February 1993 Moscow Conference offered encouraging evidence of a spirit of cooperation, but that spirit will need to be translated into concrete, collaborative efforts if evangelical Christians in the former Soviet Union are to see lasting growth fostered by their first generation of theologically trained leaders.

Notes

[1] Jack Graves, "Biblical and Theological Education Initiatives in the Former Soviet Union and Europe," unpublished directory, Overseas Council for Theological Education and Missions, 1993.

Chapter 2
Increasing Options for Theological Training in East Central Europe and Soviet Successor States (1993)

It would be difficult to identify a facet of church life that suffered more under Marxist regimes than theological education. From Siberia to the Balkans to the Baltic the majority of Orthodox, Catholic, and Protestant seminaries simply disappeared. Communists confiscated or permitted the destruction of rich libraries and archives. Faculty, not killed or arrested, rarely could continue in their calling. State authorities secularized most facilities and frequently allowed them to fall into serious disrepair. Not one of the 59 Orthodox seminaries open in Russia in 1917 survived to 1929. And the eight opened after World War II dropped to three during the Khrushchev Anti-Religious Campaign of 1959-64. Catholics in the Soviet Union were reduced to two schools and Protestants carried on without a single seminary from 1926 to 1987.

Marxists in power circumscribed and compromised the sprinkling of institutions that survived to such an extent that many faithful often felt they could not trust their own clergy. Secret police systematically interfered with faculty and administrative appointments, student admissions, and the placement of graduates. By this means atheist officials groomed a church leadership which too often was docile, morally suspect, fawning in its pronouncements of support for the state, and insensitive to grassroot complaints of religious persecution.

Reprinted with permission from *East-West Church & Ministry Report* 1 (Winter 1993): 10.

As a result of *glasnost*, the East European revolutions of 1989, and the demise of the Communist Party of the Soviet Union in 1991, East Central Europe and Soviet successor states enjoy, at least for the present, an unprecedented degree of religious liberty. A dramatic increase in the number of seminaries and seminarians all across Europe's former Communist states is one sign of faith resurgent. "Biblical and Theological Education Initiatives in the Former Soviet Union and Eastern Europe," a recent study by Jack Graves of the Overseas Council for Theological Education and Missions, documents a rapid increase in the number of seminaries and Bible institutes all across East Central Europe and the former Soviet Union. Data for schools on the territory of Soviet successor states, more complete than information currently available for East Central Europe, indicate that programs for theological training increased from 5 in 1986 to at least 54 open, or scheduled to open, by 1993:

	1986	1993
Orthodox	3	21
Catholic	2	4
Protestant	0	29

Other findings indicate that:

- At least 15 Protestant schools currently are functioning with 14 more scheduled to open by 1993;

- Evangelical training programs currently enroll at least 1,200 students;

- In addition, 2,000 more Evangelical pastors are being trained through Biblical Education by Extension (BEE), a Vienna-based consortium of 14 ministries which began working in the Soviet Union in 1988. BEE students, meeting in some 30 locations, are drawn from registered Union of Evangelical Christian-Baptist churches, autonomously registered and unregistered ECB churches, and Pentecostal, Lutheran, and Methodist churches;

- Every Evangelical school presently relies heavily on short-term Western faculty who instruct with the aid of translators;

- Very few Evangelical schools will have a majority of indigenous faculty in the foreseeable future due to past Marxist educational discrimination against believers;

- Not only faculty, but facilities, textbooks, and library collections are extremely scarce;

- To date, only the Seventh-day Adventists seem to be addressing the need for financial independence by means of an impressive agricultural work-study program;

- This study makes no attempt to identify the many short-term, seminar-type training programs currently operating.

Chapter 3

Protestant Theological Education in the Former Soviet Union, 1924-1993 (1994)

Little can be said on the subject of formal Protestant theological education for most of the Soviet era because, for almost the entire history of the USSR, it did not exist. Between 1917 and 1928 Soviet authorities closed all fifty-nine Russian Orthodox seminaries and the four Orthodox academies. Between 1944 and 1947 eight Orthodox seminaries and two academies reopened, but only three seminaries and two academies survived the Khrushchev antireligious campaign of 1959-64. Following the wartime Soviet annexation of the Baltic States, western Ukraine, and western Belorussia, the Kremlin closed almost all Catholic seminaries, allowing only one in Lithuania and one in Latvia to remain open[1]

As for Protestants, the Evangelical Christians and the Baptists jointly operated two Bible schools in Leningrad and Moscow from 1924 to 1928, while Adventists maintained two Bible schools in Kiev (1921-29) and Rostov-on-Don (1925-29). Also, in the 1970s and 1980s Lutherans had use of a small theological institute in Tallinn, Estonia. Prior to *glasnost*, that was the sum of the story.[2]

For many decades the only training available to would-be evangelical pastors was trial-and-error pulpit practice and pastoral apprenticeship under a senior presbyter. Even tutorial reading programs were extremely difficult to manage because of the scarcity of Christian literature.

Reprinted with permission from *International Bulletin of Missionary Research* 18 (January 1994): 14-16; 18-20; 22.

In 1945 newly united Evangelical Christians-Baptists (ECB) gained permission to publish *Bratskii vestnik* (Fraternal herald), the first Protestant periodical since the 1920s. General Secretary Alexander Karev and Assistant General Secretary A. I. Mitskevich saw to it that this sole publication for the ECB faithful included a maximum of didactic articles for the instruction of pastors. The initial monthly print run of 3,000 increased to 6,000 in 1974, and to 10,000 in 1978. Since for decades the circulation was too small even to provide every pastor with a subscription, each copy circulated widely. Also, it was not uncommon for *Bratskii vestnik* to be read from the pulpit prior to services.[3]

A number of ECB pastors from the Baltic States who had received Bible school or seminary training prior to Soviet annexation of their countries made significant contributions to *Bratskii vestnik* and hence to informal theological education. Estonian Oswald Tiark, with a master's of theology degree from New York's Columbia University, not only contributed to *Bratskii vestnik* but organized seminars and correspondence courses and wrote commentaries on Mark, Romans, and Ephesians, which circulated in Russian as well as Estonian.[4]

Four pastors studied at a Baptist college in England, 1957-59, and twenty-three others studied abroad in England, Germany, Sweden, and Canada from the late 1960s to 1976. But these few allowed to study abroad could in no way satisfy the huge need overall for evangelical theological education.[5]

In the 1950s the All Union Council of Evangelical Christians-Baptists (AUCECB) quietly prepared eigth mimeographed courses, which circulated secretly among selected pastors.[6] Later, in the 1960s, General Secretary Karev commissioned Alexei Bychkov, a construction engineer and future AUCECB general secretary, to translate into Russian additional materials for correspondence courses.[7] Finally, the Kremlin gave permission in 1968 for the AUCECB to launch a correspondence program. This new possibility, clearly a carrot thrown to registered churches even as dissident Baptists were feeling the stick, proved to be a major step forward however modest it might appear from a Western perspective. Texts for the new program came from the 1950s courses, from Bychkov's translations, from mimeographed *Bratskii vestnik* articles, and from Moody Bible Institute (MBI) courses.[8]

Materials from this Chicago-based institution made their way to evangelical Christians in the Soviet Union in 1961 via, of all places, Argentina. The first Russian Bible Institute in the West, which began in Benito, Manitoba, in 1942, and transferred to Toronto, Ontario, in 1943, helped launch a sister school in Rosario, Argentina, in 1944 because of the presence of three to five million Slavic immigrants in the La Plata republics (Argentina, Paraguay, and Uruguay). Konstantin Lewshenia and Mary Beechik Fewchuk, graduates of Moody Bible Institute who were teaching at the Latin American Russian Bible Institute, and Slavic Gospel Association missionaries Andrew and Pauline Semenchuk, translated MBI correspondence texts for use with their students. Here is the explanation for how essentially Arminian Evangelical Christians-Baptists came to rely heavily on works of a dispensational school for their theological education.[9]

Authorities limited correspondence enrollment to 100 per year until 1976, when the number increased to 150. By 1979, a total of 272 pastors had completed the correspondence program in dogmatic, exegetics, the Bible, pastoral theology, homiletics, church and ECB history, and the USSR constitution.[10] Nevertheless, modest state concessions to registered churches in the 1960s and 1970s could not begin to satisfy pastors' needs for a better understanding of the Bible and evangelical faith. Only in 1987 did Adventists, through arduous negotiations, secure state permission to establish a residential theological studies program.[11] Evangelicals' pent-up frustrations over seven decades of varying combinations of persecution, repression, and discrimination exploded between 1990 and 1992 in a frenzy of activity leading to the founding of some forty-four additional programs of theological education.[12] With few exceptions these Protestant Bible schools and seminaries still lack texts, libraries, permanent faculties, and permanent facilities. Nevertheless, they possess staff with exceptional dedication, infectious enthusiasm, and high hopes, and their students are extraordinarily eager to learn. Many Western seminaries with incomparably greater material assets, would be justified in being envious.

Profile of the Present Situation

Nineteen Protestant residential Bible schools and seminaries report 1,667 students currently enrolled in programs of at least one year in length. The eight largest institutions have 100 to 220 students each, while the next eleven in size enroll 18 to 75 students each. (See Appendix.) These figures do not account for scores of institutions for which enrollment data are not yet available. Nor do they include well over 1,000 students receiving instruction in three-week to six-month courses (Victory Bible Institute and Korean Methodist Bible School).[13] And they do not include over three thousand pastors studying by correspondence in at least five programs.

The level of instruction in the new residential schools, in the majority of cases, approximates that received in Western, freshman-level college or university courses, simply because few believers under Communism had a chance to receive a university education. An increasing number of new believers with higher education may change this if, as seems likely, they enter seminaries in increasing numbers.

Protestant theological programs, not surprisingly, tend to be concentrated in larger cities, with the capitals of Moscow, Kiev, and Riga having especially strong enrollments. Several programs have moved, or are moving, to St. Petersburg and Kiev from smaller cities; Logos from Belorechensk to St. Petersburg; St. James from Koresten to Kiev; and Donetsk Bible College from Donetsk to Kiev.

Ukrainian institutions command attention because of their disproportionately large number and size. Ukrainians in the former Soviet Union number 52 million, whereas Russians number 147 million, yet Ukraine has slightly more Protestant seminary students than Russia (606 versus 595). Also, Kiev, which is a fraction of Moscow's size, has a third more Protestant seminary students (381 compared to 281, if the Donetsk school, which is moving to Kiev, is counted in the totals). And Moscow's largest Protestant institution is only the eighth largest in the former Soviet Union.

Before the breakup of the USSR, the strength of Orthodox, Catholic, and Protestant churches in Ukraine led William Fletcher to label it the Bible Belt of the Soviet Union.[14] For example, nearly 50 percent of Adventists in the former USSR reside in Ukraine, versus 21 percent in Russia; 50 percent of Evangelical Christians-Baptists reside in Ukraine, versus 33 percent in Russia; and 67 percent of Pentecostals reside in Ukraine, versus 3 percent in Russia.[15] Yet the striking concentration of believers in Ukraine is not matched with available Christian literature, either in terms of quantities published in-country or in terms of materials imported from the West. In 1987-88, for example, only 8 percent of the copies of Scripture published in, or imported into, the USSR were in the Ukrainian language. And in 1992 the United Bible Societies imported two and a half times as many Scriptures and Scripture portions into Russia as they did into Ukraine (1,999,581 versus 777,202).[16] Assuming that Christian literature in general is being supplied in the same proportions, it is easy to see the added burden Ukrainian institutions face in procuring texts and in developing libraries.

As for denominational affiliation, the new schools include some 535 Pentecostal and 530 Baptist students. Lutherans, with over a half million members, would appear to have the least favorable ratio of seminarians to membership. Conversely, Adventists, with approximately 80,000 members, have the most favorable ratio of seminarians to membership.

Even though this investigation focuses on residential centers, it should be noted that a majority of pastors presently are receiving their training through correspondence courses, which will probably be true for several years to come.

Correspondence Program	No. Enrolled
Bible Education by Extension (BEE), including 700 ECB pastors in the Russian Republic	2,000
International Correspondence Institute (Pentecostal)	714
Moscow Correspondence Bible Institute	200
Lutheran Theological Institute	100
Apocalypse (Logos-related interdenominational program in Krasnodar)	90
Adventist	80
Total	3,184

Higher costs for residential programs, the size of the country, transportation problems, and the difficulty pastors with church and family responsibilities face in leaving home for extended periods necessitate the continuation of strong correspondence programs, at least in the near term.[17] Still, residential programs are in great demand. Many schools can accommodate only a small portion of their applicants.

Priorities of National Seminaries

On February 11, 1993, the Overseas Council for Theological Education and Missions, Peter Deyneka Russian Ministries, and Wheaton College's Institute for East-West Christian Studies sponsored a conference in Moscow attended by thirty-eight Russians and Ukrainians representing twenty-two new Protestant Bible schools and seminaries. In that meeting seminary delegates expressed more concern for quality, affordable course texts than they did for any other need.[18] For example, Anatolii Glukhovskii of the New Life Theological School in Kiev reported that his students currently had texts for only seven of fifteen courses.[19]

A number of challenges face those who would seek to remedy this shortage:

1. As yet, no single master list exists for Christian titles available in the various languages of the former Soviet Union.

2. Nor does a clearinghouse exist to provide bibliographic control for translations in progress. The potential for waste (and for confusion over copyright issues) was illustrated at the February theological education conference as two schools (Zaoksky and Odessa) reported that each recently had completed translations of William Sanford LaSor's *Old Testament Survey*.[20]

3. Most titles available in translation are not presently in print, or available copies cannot begin to service present seminary needs.

4. Fewer than 400 Protestant works have been in print in Russian in recent years, and fewer than 100 Protestant titles in Ukrainian.[21] Historians often note that the Reformation had little or no impact in sixteenth- and seventeenth-century Russia, with ramifications to the present day. For example, only in 1992-93 were such Protestant classics as John Calvin's Institutes of the Christian Religion and John Wesley's Standard Sermons being translated into Russian.[22]

5. Available titles would be suitable for only a limited number of classes, since most are devotional or evangelistic in nature.

6. A number of delegates at the February 1993 conference noted that the quality of translations too often is poor.

7. Many schools as yet lack a sufficiently broad exposure to the range of evangelical literature to ensure the choice of the best texts for varying purposes and levels of instruction.

If texts are in short supply, libraries must be but a dream. Compared with the St. Petersburg Orthodox Seminary and Academy Library, with 300,000 volumes, the largest Protestant collection is the Zoaksky Adventist Seminary, with 12,000 volumes.[23] Other collections presently exist only as projections, or number in the hundreds, or have hefty percentages of less accessible English-language works or less relevant non-theological titles.

If few pastors as yet have had the benefit of a seminary education, it is to be expected that individuals qualified to teach in Protestant seminaries would be especially rare. Consequently, for the time being, every Protestant seminary in the former Soviet Union is relying heavily upon instructors from the West. The vast majority of the guest lecturers teach through interpreters. According to seminary representatives at the February conference, in addition to this handicap, many Western instructors lack sufficient appreciation for Russian, Ukrainian, and Baltic history and culture, a problem that better orientation could help to correct.[24]

For years to come a serious obstacle to contextualized Protestant theological education in the former Soviet Union will be the lack of indigenous believers qualified for seminary teaching positions. Consequently, the question of how best to prepare Russian, Ukrainian, and Baltic seminary faculty deserves careful study. In recent decades a lack of judicious screening of students for seminary study in Europe and North America has precipitated a crippling Third World theological brain drain. The percentage of seminarians not returning from study abroad is estimated to be as high as 75 percent from Colombia, 85 percent from the Caribbean, and 90 percent from India.[25] It is hoped that Western seminaries will keep this danger in mind as they accept students from Soviet successor states.[26]

Principles for Moving Forward

Many church leaders in the former Soviet Union already have concluded that lengthy study abroad may prove counterproductive, even assuming students return home. For example, in a recent survey of Protestant theological educators in the former Eastern bloc, World Vision Germany director Manfred Kohl discovered overwhelming support for training in-country and great wariness concerning the consequences of study abroad. (Of forty-eight respondents, twenty-three favored in-country residence programs, twenty-four favored correspondence courses, and only one favored study abroad.) In his 1992 interviews Kohl noted consistent opposition to theological training in the West, which was expressed "very politely, but very strongly."[27] It thus behooves educators and church leaders, East and West, to proceed with caution.

The following six suggestions seem best to take account of present needs and also risks:

1. Encourage study abroad only for especially talented, mature, and dedicated pastors targeted for teaching positions, preferably those who would not bring their families with them to the West. The costs entailed in more trips home would be preferable to the financial and cultural costs of family residence in the West.

2. Utilize extension programs and competency tests to shorten the length of Western instruction.

3. Encourage completion of M.A. programs, rather than longer M.Div. programs or doctoral programs. Doctorates probably will be desired more than they will be needed for at least the first decade of residential seminary education in the former Soviet Union.

4. Encourage Western church and parachurch groups and seminaries and the churches of the former Soviet Union to join forces in establishing perhaps a single Russian and a single Ukrainian graduate-level Protestant theological program in order to foster the contextualization of seminary education and to minimize the theological brain drain.

5. Encourage Western institutions to work together in strengthening a few graduate-level programs in the former Soviet Union by means of coordinated faculty postings in the East and cooperative credit from Western degree programs.

6. Invest more resources in Western faculty teaching in the East, especially those with relevant language skills, and less in student scholarships for study in the West.

At the February theological education conference, seminary representatives emphasized their concerns for (1) an organization to facilitate ongoing sharing of information and coordination, (2) permanent facilities, (3) financial support, and (4) the establishment of seminary accreditation standards. Delegates hoped for help from abroad through a process of East-West interaction, rather than Western dictation. Indeed, the issue of outside assistance, and how best to effect it, is bound to loom large. Comments to this effect in Kohl's theological education survey make this clear:

- We want to know what is going on…what is available.

- How can we become part of the loop?

- We are hungry and thirsty for information and fellowship.

- We do not want everything to be given to us, but we must know what is available.

- We do not want ready-made Western Christianity to be dumped on us. We would love to have the tools, and then we will work it out for ourselves.[28]

Prudent assistance from abroad will focus on aid that will minimize long-term dependency. To date, unfortunately, only Adventists seem to have taken this concern to heart. Their Zaoksky Seminary includes a fifty-five-acre farm, greenhouses, a canning plant, and a printing press, which not only supply the needs of their community but produce revenue for the support of the institution. Most theological education programs not only lack income-producing auxiliary services but also feel obligated to abide by the long-standing, even pre-Revolution, custom of awarding student stipends above and beyond the Western practice of tuition scholarships. The lack of part-time or summer employment for students, compounded by growing unemployment and inflation, does not help the problem.[29]

Information sharing and greater coordination will be vital if evangelical Christians are to avoid working at cross-purposes, as in the case of indigenous versus Western study, and to avoid needless duplication, as in the case of the two translations of the same Old Testament textbook. Yet meaningful cooperation will be a daunting task, even assuming that both parties, East and West, see the benefit. To start with, the numbers alone compound the challenge of working together. Twenty-five indigenous Protestant denominations[30] and close to a thousand indigenous parachurch missions and charities now function in the former Soviet Union.[31] Also, approximately 700 Western church and parachurch ministries currently work in East Central Europe and the former Soviet Union.[32] No less than fifty Western organizations are assisting new Protestant schools. At the Moscow theological education conference alone forty-six representatives of twenty-seven different Western church and parachurch bodies gathered for the day.

The February meeting provided a helpful illustration of evangelical, but otherwise doctrinally diverse, groups working together. Evangelical Christian-Baptist, Pentecostal, Mennonite, Adventist, and Presbyterian delegates chose to stress their common concerns for training and equipping leaders rather than their theological differences. And Western participants chose to listen at length to the priorities of Russian and Ukrainian representatives rather than recite what the West thought best.

Indigenous and Western leaders working together took the following concrete steps:

1. National delegates formed four committees to continue discussions on literature development (for course texts and libraries), faculty development, a future theological education conference, and information sharing and coordination.

2. Delegates appointed a small group of Russians and Ukrainians to work with Dr. Peter Kuzmic of the Evangelical Theological Institute, Osijek, Croatia, to help organize a 1994 conference

on theological education in East Central Europe and Soviet successor states.

3. Peter Deyneka Russian Ministries volunteered to organize a representative committee to select twenty texts already available in Russian that would be reprinted for 1993-94 classes. (The Overseas Council will administer a grant awarded in June 1993 for the purpose of launching the reprint project. Full funding would involve the reprinting of twenty texts per year for five years.)

4. Peter Deyneka Russian Ministries agreed to coordinate a comprehensive Christian literature survey project, including evaluations, with the assistance of David C. Cook Foundation, Mission Forum's Literature Information Service, and Wheaton Colege's Institute for East-West Christian Studies.[33]

5. The Christian Resource Center, Moscow, agreed to provide administrative oversight for a projected theological library that would not be associated with any one denomination but would be open to all seminary students, including Orthodox and Catholic, as a means of bridge-building. Copies of works collected in the Russian Ministries survey project would be deposited in the new Moscow library, at an as yet undermined institution in Kiev, and in the Billy Graham Center Library at Wheaton College. (A grant proposal is pending for the development of the Moscow and Kiev theological collections.)

Projections

Finally, a number of projections would seem reasonably safe to make, notwithstanding the fluid and volatile politics and economics of Soviet successor states.

1. In all probability, correspondence programs, as noted, will continue to service many students, especially if economic conditions continue to deteriorate.

2. Continuing political decentralization and fragmentation and growing nationalism will make it increasingly problematic for individual seminaries to draw students from many republics. Simply put, crossing borders may grow ever more difficult. The Russian Orthodox Seminary and Academy in St. Petersburg and Zaoksky Adventist Seminary already see this as a significant problem.

3. The need for more Christian literature in Ukrainian will increase. Even if 21 percent of Ukraine's population is Russian, and even if a majority of students in Ukraine can study in Russian, will they want to? Should they have to? Over time, will it be politic for schools there to depend on Russian-language instruction?[34]

4. For better or worse, assistance from abroad will prove vital in the development of residential programs (which require literature, libraries, faculty, and buildings), just as it was vital in the development of correspondence programs earlier.

5. Generational tensions in church leadership likely will be heightened with better-educated younger pastors and laypeople seeing church life differently from older leaders and laity, who outlived the state assault without benefit of education.

6. Finally, nondenominational schools (with an enrollment of 366 at present) are likely to grow in importance as Western and indigenous parachurch groups plant more and more churches that are neither Baptist nor Pentecostal, *per se*.[35]

Protestant theological education is emerging in the former Soviet Union in a manner unique in the history of Reformation churches. Never before, and nowhere else, have Protestants launched as many formal theological training programs as rapidly as they have in Soviet successor states—and what is doubly unprecedented, they started from a base of zero. Much that is positive can be said for the vision, enthusiasm, and energy of the new theological educators in the East, and for the willingness of an array of Western evangelical church and parachurch agencies to assist. At the same time, sober reflection would suggest that too many institutions have been founded without sufficient consideration (1) for the advisability of collaborative efforts in the expensive and labor-intensive areas of faculty, text, and library development; and (2) for the need to ponder the pitfalls and lessons to be gleaned from the history or Protestant theological education. Seminaries in Soviet successor states should consider carefully Western models and Western money and what both entail. Western involvement could sap vitality, foster dependency, and replicate the debilitating Third World-First World theological brain drain, if assistance is not measured, culturally nuanced, and carefully coordinated.

The February 1993 Moscow Conference on Theological Education offered encouraging evidence of a spirit of cooperation, both among indigenous churches and seminaries, and between them and Western participants. That spirit will need to be translated into many concrete, collaborative efforts if evangelical Christians in the former Soviet Union are to see lasting growth fostered by its first generation of theologically trained leaders.

Notes

The author's notes from meetings and interviews held in February and March 1993 proved helpful at a number of points. Sources include Peter Deyneka, Jr., Anatolii Glukhovskii, Ludmilla Gorbuzova, Jack Graves, Terry Henshaw, Manfred Kohl, Anne-Marie Kool, Mikhail Kulakov, Jr., Peter Penner, Heigo Ritsbek, Terry Schnake, Andrew Semenchuk, Igor Tsiupak, and Charles Warner.

[1] Dimitry Pospielovsky, *The Russian Church Under the Soviet Regime, 1917-1982*, vol. 2 (Crestwood, N.Y.: St. Vladimir's Seminary Press, 1984), p. 302; A. Johansen, *Theological Study in the Russian and Bulgarian Orthodox Churches Under Communist Rule* (London: Faith Press, 1963), p. 4.

[2] Mark Elliott, "Seventh-Day Adventists in Russia and the Soviet Union," in *Modern Encyclopedia of Russian and Soviet History*, vol. 34, pp. 111-12; Walter Sawatsky, *Soviet Evangelicals Since World War II* (Scottdale, PA: Herald Press, 1981), pp. 46, 331; Heigo Ritsbek interview, November 14, 1991. The crippling effect of long-standing state proscription of Protestant theological education appears somewhat less debilitating when contrasted with the pervasive KGB interference in the life of the three token Orthodox seminaries that survived the Khrushchev antireligious campaign. State manipulation of evangelical pastors may have been less successful overall simply because Protestants lacked seminaries. See Jane Ellis, *The Russian Orthodox Church: A Contemporary History* (Bloomington: Indiana University Press, 1986), pp. 109-20; and Anthony Ugolnik, *The Orthodox Church and Contempory Politics in the USSR* (Washington, D.C.: National Council for Soviet and East European Research, 1991), pp. 21-24.

[3] Sawatsky, *Soviet Evangelicals*, pp. 331, 425.

[4] *Ibid.*, p. 331.

[5] *Ibid.*, pp. 330-31; Alexander de Chalandeau, "The Theology of the Evangelical Christians-Baptists in the USSR. As Reflected in the *Bratskii Vestnik*" (Ph.D. diss., University of Strasbourg, 1978), pp. 43-45.

[6] Peter Deyneka, Jr., in William S. Covington, Jr., "Consultation on Theological Education in the Former Soviet Union, A Conference at Wheaton College," Minutes, September 3, 1992.

[7] Chalandeau, "Theology," p. 41; "Rev. Alexei Bychkov and Rev. Michael Zhidkov Sharing with Wheaton Area Pastors," transcript, March 13, 1987, p. 6.

[8] Sawatsky, *Soviet Evangelicals*, pp. 330-31; Chalandeau, "Theology," p. 45.

[9] Andrew Semenchuk was president of RBI from 1955 to 1968. The Toronto school was a joint venture of Oswald J. Smith, Toronto People's Church, and Peter Deyneka,

Sr., Slavic Gospel Association. The Toronto school closed about 1954 (Semenchuk in Covington, "Consultation," p. 2; Semenchuk interview, March 17, 1993).

[10] Sawatsky, *Soviet Evangelicals*, p. 330; Chalandeau, "Theology," pp. 45-46. The state also required Orthodox seminaries to study the USSR constitution. For the Orthodox course of study, see Johansen, *Theological Study*, pp. 4-5; and Ellis, *Russian Orthodox*, p. 116.

[11] Marite Sapiets, *True Witness: The Story of Seventh-Day Adventists in the Soviet Union* (Keston, England: Keston College, 1990), p. 286; Mikhail Kulakov, Jr., interview, February 15, 1993; Mikhail Kulakov, Jr., "Zaoksky Theological Seminary, Presenting to You Our Seminary," unpublished flier (1992).

[12] Jack Graves, "Biblical and Theological Education Initiatives in the Former Soviet Union and Eastern Europe," unpublished directory, Overseas Council for Theological Education and Missions, 1993, p. 1; interviews with Jack Graves and Manfred Kohl. There are now eighteen Orthodox and eight Catholic seminaries.

[13] Interview in St. Petersburg with Terry Henshaw, February 9, 1993; interview in Moscow with Ludmilla Gorbuzova, February 14, 1993. A survey of theological educators in East Central Europe and the former Soviet Union, undertaken by World Vision Germany director Manfred Kohl, revealed that 25 of 51 respondents favored three-year programs, 13 favored two-year programs, but only 2 favored one-year programs ("Towards Globalization of Theological Education: Feasibility Study on Extending Theological Education into Eastern Europe and Parts of the Former USSR," Survey Appendix [thesis prospectus, Gordon Conwell Theological Seminary, October 15, 1992], p. 1). In contrast, Russian Orthodox seminary and academy courses run four years each (Johansen, *Theological Study*, p. 4).

[14] William Fletcher, "The Soviet Bible Belt: World War II's Impact on Relitgon," in *The Impact of World War II on the Soviet Union*, ed. Susan J. Linz (New York: Rowan and Allanheld, 1985).

[15] Kent Hill, *The Soviet Union on the Brink: An Inside Look at Christianity and Glasnost* (Portland, OR: Multnomah Press, 1991), p. 373; Sapiets, *True Witness*, pp. 274-78; Philip Walters, *World Christianity: Eastern Europe* (Monrovia, CA: MARC, 1988), p. 72; Walter Sawatsky, "Protestantism in the USSR," in *Religious Policy in the Soviet Union*, ed. Sabrina Ramet (Cambridge: Cambridge University Press, 1991), pp. 18-19; Ralph Mann, "Soviet Pentecostal Demographics," unpublished paper (Denton, TX: Mission Possible, October 1991), p. 2.

[16] Mark Elliott, "New Openness in USSR Prompts Massive Bible Shipments to Soviet Christians in 1987-88: A Statistical Overview," *News Network International*, March 20, 1989, p. 28; idem, "Scripture Imports to Former Eastern Bloc," *United Bible Societies World Report* 271 (March, 1993): 30.

¹⁷ Chuck Schwartz, BEE, speaking at Moscow Theological Education Conference, February 11, 1993; fax from Beth Yost, International Correspondence Institute, March 17, 1993; author's notes from reports at Moscow Theological Education Conference, February 11, 1993; interview with Anne Kull, Lutheran School of Theology, Chicago, March 29, 1993; Kohl, "Towards Globalization," pp. 17, 24-25; Mikhail Kulakov (February 15, 1993, interview) noted that 500 Adventists also were studying theological education by extension at three sites.

¹⁸ Fourteen of twenty-four respondents listed the need for texts as the most urgent. See Jack Graves, "Report of the Conference on Theological Education in the Former Soviet Union, Moscow, Russia, February 10-12, 1993," Overseas Council for Theological Education and Missions, February 24, 1993, p. 2.

¹⁹ Author's notes from February 11, 1993, Moscow Conference. The Orthodox have had to contend with the same shortage. See Ellis, *Russian Orthodox*, p. 108.

²⁰ David Allan Hubbard and Frederick William Bush assisted La Sor in revising his *Old Testament Survey: The Message, Form, and Background of the Old Testament* (Grand Rapids, MI: Wm. B. Eerdmans Publishing Co., 1982). Odessa holds the Russian translation rights.

²¹ *Books Translated from English to Eastern European and CIS Languages* (Elgin, IL: Davic C. Cook Foundation, 1992) includes 370 Russian titles and 51 Ukrainian titles.

²² Christian Bridge, Carol Stream, IL, translated into Russian H. Henry Meeter's *Basic Ideas of Calvinism* and is overseeing the Russian translation in Moscow of *The Golden Book of Calvinism*, an abridgement of the *Institutes*. Funders include the Christian Reformed Church World Literature Ministries and the Back to God Hour. Calvin's *Institutes* previously did circulate in East Central Europe in Latin. Rev. George Rodonaia, a United Methodist pastor in Houston, Texas, originally from Soviet Georgia, translated the *Standard Sermons*, which may be published in Moscow by Golden Age Publishing House.

²³ Author's conversations with St. Petersburg Vice-Rector Veniamin, February 8, 1993, and Adventist seminary president, Mikhail Kulakov, Jr., February 15, 1993. See also Ellis, *Russian Orthodox*, p. 107.

²⁴ Nine of twenty-four conference respondents cited faculty development as a critical concern (author's notes from February 11, 1993, Moscow Conference). See also Kohl, "Towards Globalization," pp. 22-23. Sawatsky (*Soviet Evangelicals*, p. 330) heads his section on theological education, "The Missing Teachers."

²⁵ Jack Graves, "Plugging the Theological Brain Drain," *Evangelical Missions Quarterly* 28 (April 1992), p. 155. See also "Bring Training In, Not People Out," *Albanian Insight*, No. 20 (February 27, 1992), p. 2.

²⁶ Students from the former Soviet Union currently are enrolled at Asbury Theological Seminary, Dallas Theological Seminary, Denver Conservative Baptist Seminary, Fuller Theological Seminary, Mennonite Brethren Biblical Seminary, Moody Bible Institute, Southern Baptist Seminary, Southwestern Baptist Theological Seminary, and Wheaton College.

²⁷ Kohl, "Towards Globalization," p. 1 (survey appendix), p. 16 (text).

²⁸ *Ibid.*, pp. 20-21 (text).

²⁹ James W. Cunningham, *A Vanquished Hope: The Movement for Church Renewal in Russia, 1905-1906* (Crestwood, N.Y.: St. Vladimir's Seminary Press, 1981), p. 47; Ellis, *Russian Orthodox*, p. 105; Graves, "Biblical and Theological Initiatives in the Former Soviet Union and Eastern Europe," unpublished directory, Overseas Council for Theological Education and Missions, 1992, p. 2.

³⁰ Twenty-one denominations are listed in Mark Elliott and Robert Richardson, "Growing Protestant Diversity in the Former Soviet Union," in *Russian Pluralism, Now Irreversible?* Ed. Uri Ra'anan et al. (New York: St. Martin's Press 1992), p. 204. Four additional denominations now working in the former Soviet Union are Christian and Missionary Alliance, Pentecostal Holiness, Christian Reformed, and Evangelical Covenant.

³¹ Author's conversations with Dr. Sharon Linzey, Moscow State University visiting professor, February 15, 1993.

³² Sharon Linzey, Holt Ruffin, and Mark Elliott, eds., *East-West Christian Organizations Directory* (Evanston, IL: Berry Publishing Services, 1993), includes 687 entries. The author has files on an additional 35.

³³ Wil Triggs and Mark Elliott, "Christian Literature: Who Has Published What, Where, and in Which Languages:" *East-West Church & Ministry Report* 1 (Spring 1993): 12.

³⁴ Michael Mandelbaum, ed., *The Rise of Nations in the Soviet Union* (New York: Council of Foreign Relations, 1991), p. 103.

³⁵ Elliott and Richardson, "Growing Protestant Diversity," pp. 198-200.

Appendix

Name	Affiliation*	Date of Founding	Location	Enrollment
Calvary Bible Institute	P	Jan. 1991	Riga, Latvia	220
Zaoksky Theological Seminary**	A	1987	Zaoksky, Russia	170
Odessa Bible College and Theological Seminary**	ECB	Oct. 1991	Odessa, Ukraine	160
St. James Bible College	N (75%P)	Apr. 1991	Kiev, Ukraine	132
Baptist Theological Seminary**	ECB	1991	Kiev	129
Logos Christian College**	N	Oct. 1990	St. Petersburg, Russia	114
Riga Lutheran Seminary	L	-	Riga	110
Victory Theological Institute**	P	Oct. 1992	Moscow, Russia	102
Bible Training School** ***	P	Oct. 1991	Moscow	75
Lutheran Theological Institute	L	-	Tallinn, Estonia	70
Theological Seminary of Christians of Evangelical Faith**	P	1990	Ternopol, Ukraine	65
New Life Theological School**	N	Aug. 1992	Kiev	62
Donetsk Bible College**	N	1991	Donetsk, Ukraine	58
Moscow Theological Institute**	P	Oct. 1992	Moscow	54
Baptist Training Center**	ECB	1991	Moscow	50
Temple of the Gospel Seminary	ECB	Mar. 1991	St. Petersburg	30

Theological Faculty, University of Tartu	L	-	Tartu, Estonia	28
Latvian Baptist Seminary	ECB	-	Riga	20
Estonian Baptist Seminary	ECB	Oct. 1989	Tartu	18

Total   1,667

*Denominational affiliations are as follows: A- Adventist,
ECB= Evangelical Christian-Baptist, L= Lutheran;
N= Nondenominational, and P= Pentecostal.
**Represented at the Moscow conference on theological education, February 1992.
***Sponsored by Bethany World Prayer Center and Gulf States Mission Agency.

SECTION 2
ESTABLISHING A SOLID FOUNDATION

CHAPTER 4
AFTER COMMUNISM: THE MIXED BLESSING OF WESTERN ASSISTANCE (1995)

In the summer of 1994 staff of St. Petersburg Christian University, which in fact is a seminary, sifted through literally tons of books donated from the West, ferreting out the occasional title relevant for a theological library. On the one hand, the task required time consuming sorting through mountains of boxes for the relatively rare gems in the rough. On the other hand, the shipping had been donated, several thousand useful titles were being gleaned from the heap, and seminarians would make use of a fair portion of the rest that the school would pass over. And so it is with Western assistance to theological education in the East, writ large: a mixed blessing. The question is how help should not be given, and how help should and should not be received.

In February 1993 Overseas Council for Theological Education and Missions, Peter Deyneka Russian Ministries, and Wheaton College's Institute for East-West Christian Studies hosted a meeting of evangelical educators in Moscow. Insights drawn from that conference, plus seminary site visits and library research, served as the basis for a survey of the current state of Protestant theological education in the former Soviet Union. Three findings of that investigation follow.

1. Prior to *glasnost* formal Protestant theological education was practically nonexistent. However, under Gorbachev an explosion

---

This paper was delivered at the Consultation on Theological Education and Leadership Development in Post-Communist Europe, Oradea, Romania, 4 October 1994. Reprinted with permission from *The Asbury Theological Journal* 50 (Spring 1995): 67-73.

of pent-up energy and demand saw well over 40 residential programs established in three years (1990-1992). These schools have emerged "in a manner unique in the history of Reformation churches. Never before, and nowhere else, have Protestants launched as many formal theological training programs as rapidly as they have in Soviet successor states.[1]

2. The new seminaries and training centers possess unusually dedicated staff and extraordinarily eager students, but the vast majority of the schools lack sufficient texts, adequate libraries, qualified faculty, and permanent facilities.

3. At the present time programs, representing several thousand residential students and several thousand additional extension and correspondence students, depend very heavily upon Western assistance. This third point serves as the focus of the present study.

How Western help is managed—or mismanaged—will make a major difference in the ability—or inability—of new schools to strengthen the Church in the East and to assist the Church as it seeks to witness to an enormous number of nonbelievers in its midst.

"We do not want ready-made Western Christianity to be dumped on us," a Russian theological educator reported in 1992. "We would love to have the tools, and then we will work it out ourselves."[2] While such sentiments abound among post-Soviet bloc seminary administrators, paradoxically, Ralph Alexander of Biblical Education by Extension rightly characterizes the present fixation of these same leaders on Western accreditation as an "obsession."[3]

What does this readily observable striving for Western credentials portend and how might it foster rather than deter the manufacture of "ready-made Western Christianity" east of the old Iron Curtain? Russian church historian Walter Sawatsky has predicted that, particularly among evangelical Protestants, "the dominant literature in theology, and even the dominant theories for theological education will likely be drawn from North America," at the expense of training that is "contextually Slavic."[4] While the new Russian Protestant Euro-Asiatic Accreditation Association hosted a conference in October 1994 on the history of "The Protestant Movement in Russia" without Western participation, it appears, at the same time, that this body is likely to adopt wholesale Western criteria for the evaluation and credentialing of evangelical seminaries in the former Soviet Union.[5]

Western standards may be desirable in terms of required instructional facilities, faculty with earned doctorates, libraries of sufficient size and quality, and a broad curriculum. But for the foreseeable future such criteria are prohibitively expensive, beyond the reach of the vast majority of institutions in former Soviet bloc countries. Even worse, uncritical acceptance of Western standards, what Regent College professor Paul Stevens calls "slavish replication of Western curriculum and educational philosophy," would unquestionably doom theological education in former East bloc countries to abject economic dependence upon the West, and with it, *de facto* foreign control."[6]

Furthermore, to the extent that Western credentialing favors academic accomplishment over pastoral training and ministry, it may actually undermine, rather than facilitate, Christian leadership training after communism. How so? If Western accreditation standards prevail, it quickly becomes apparent that at present the "right" credentials can only be had in the West, hence the scramble for study abroad, Western degrees, and what might be termed "bright flight."

Manfred Kohl's survey of theological educators in the East documented "overwhelming support for training in-country."[7] But the decline in Soviet-style central church authority and the lure of the West already is spelling more and more post-Soviet seminarians opting for golden opportunities abroad. Borrowing from an American folk-song, "Will they ever return," or will they "ride forever neath the streets of Boston?" Past performance suggests another brain drain could be in the making. Seventy-five percent of Colombian theological students who have studied abroad never have gone home, the same for 85 percent of seminarians from the Caribbean and 90 percent of seminarians from India.[8] Is there any reason to believe it will be otherwise with East bloc seminarians?

Wilson Chow, president of Hong Kong's China Graduate School of Theology, just returned from the former Yugoslavia, already reports a "brain-drain of the theologically trained because of internal ethnic conflicts, the unstable political situation, [and] the attraction from seminaries in the West."[9] The present priority of North America's Association of Theological Schools upon globalization provides a perfect example of a Western academic standard being unhealthy and counter-productive for theological education elsewhere.[10] In the name of diversity and globalization too many Western seminaries currently are luring to their campuses rare, theologically trained seminary educators from abroad, often draining the lifeblood of struggling institutions. How ironic that Western seminaries could be so insensitive to the damage they may inflict upon schools outside the North Atlantic community—all in the name of a better understanding of the rest of the world!

Even if every theological student in the West did return home, unhealthy side effects still might cause the church in the East to question the advisability of study abroad. As Ralph Alexander points out, when seminarians study in another country, "training is removed from the normal context."[11] In addition, seminarians' introduction to Western living standards and Western cultural values makes going home a difficult adjustment. The negative influences of narcissistic materialism and individualism are self-evident. But even defensible Western mores, such as the high premium placed on efficiency, productivity, and punctuality, pose problems for graduates attempting to re-enter societies that frequently value the building of relationships more highly than the completion of tasks by a set date. Also, modern higher criticism of the Scriptures, a staple of Western theological education—even in evangelical institutions reacting to it—will not be a welcome import in the eyes of a great many church leaders east of the old Iron Curtain.[12]

The intense yearning of theological educators in the East for academic respectability actually could undermine effective leadership development. As Yugoslav theologian Peter Kuzmic argues, "We cannot uncritically copy Western models where truth is separated from practice and where the world of academia is separated from the world of ecclesia. Instead of being accountable to the church, religious truth becomes a selfish, elitist, academic exercise."[13] In the same vein, theology professor Paul Stevens warns that "pride in degrees and publishing records" can lead to "the loss of humility as a Christian goal."[14] Both a respect for learning and a fear of learning—lest it replace a fear of the Lord—should stand side by side to prevent the one from breeding unbridled pride or the other from breeding mindless anti-intellectualism.

In the West programs exist which focus on the imparting of knowledge, or the formation of character, or practical and experiential preparation for ministry, or some combination of the three. Already in the East some of the same tendencies find expression. For example, the Evangelical Baptist Theological Seminary in Odessa appears to have the greatest emphasis upon academic scholarship of any Protestant institution in the former Soviet Union, while Donetsk Bible College stresses missions, ministry skills, and "experience-based learning with existing new churches."[15] At a February 1992 meeting on leadership training in Vienna, Austria, Greg Reader of International Teams stressed that "theological education should be accountable to the context it serves."[16] It would appear that an effective application of this principle may be observed at Donetsk: students maintain close, ongoing ties with local churches.

It can be argued that the lengthier and the more extensive theological education becomes, the greater the danger that it will increase the distance between pulpit and pew. Theological educators in the East should note that this "clergy-lay problem" requires conscious, ongoing, creative attention, and that the West is hardly the place to look for its solution.[17] (Ironically, the Kremlin's longstanding prohibition against Protestant theological education led to an ad *hoc* apprenticeship system of pastoral training, the unintended positive effect of which was to minimize the distance between clergy and laity.)

A final reason indiscriminate emulation of Western theological education would be unwise is that the West itself is increasingly unsure of the validity of its own approach, which one detractor has described as the "trained incapacity to deal with the real problems of actual living persons in their daily lives." Oddly enough, the world seems to crave this "desert experience...at the very moment when leaders in Western theological education are having serious misgivings about their enterprise."[18]

A seminary student studying in North America once asked, "How is it that the only form of theological education that has been given to us in Africa comes from the part of the world where the church is in decline?" An equally pointed rejoinder could have been, "How is it that, knowing the church in the West is in decline, African denominations are so hungry to get this sort of ministerial training that the West offers?"[19]

From a distance few can detect the disarray to be found in many Western churches and seminaries, especially through the rich camouflage of institutional endowments, bricks and mortar, and the flood of Christian books, videos, conferences, and the like. On the other hand, the global commitment and material prosperity of many Western evangelical churches, missions, and seminaries has translated into an extraordinary, perhaps unprecedented outpouring of assistance for fledgling seminaries and Bible institutes all across East Central Europe and the former Soviet Union. In most institutions Western assistance is welcome. The question is what kind of assistance is beneficial and who would make that decision.

If the case has been made that the Western connection to Christian leadership development in the East is a mixed blessing, what recommendations might contribute to more enlightened Western assistance.

1. Theological educators in East Central Europe and the former Soviet Union should be encouraged to develop culture-specific criteria for evaluating the effectiveness of leadership training programs. They should be creative and judicious in adapting, rather than submitting to the wholesale adoption of, Western accrediting standards. They should weigh carefully the costs of accepting secular governments as the accrediting agents for theological schools. And they should look worldwide for innovative approaches to the evaluation of programs and graduates, such as those Jack Graves of Overseas Council for Theological Education has identified in Brazil and Indonesia.

2. They should have close institutional, faculty, and student interaction with the local church.[20] Churches do not exist in order to support seminaries. But seminaries should exist in order to support churches.

3. They should stress the importance of theological training in-country, for all the previously discussed cultural, theological, and economic reasons. To that end seminaries in former Soviet bloc states should:

a. Encourage study abroad only for especially talented, mature, and dedicated pastors targeted for teaching positions;

b. Shorten the length of Western instruction, utilize extension programs and competency tests, and encourage completion of M.A. programs, rather than longer M. Div. or doctoral programs;

c. Encourage Western and indigenous churches, missions, and seminaries to work together in a few in-country advanced degree programs;

d. Encourage Western partners to invest more resources in Western faculty teaching in the East, especially those with relevant language skills, and less video talking heads and student scholarships for study in the West.[21]

e. Also, before opting for West European or North American theological education, students from East Central Europe and the former Soviet Union should consider alternatives in non-Western nations that would entail much less culture shock and theological dissonance, at a fraction of the cost. For example, the South Asia Institute of Advance Christian Studies, Bangalore, India, would welcome students from East Central Europe and the former Soviet Union in its fully accredited programs for pastoral training or advanced degrees for future theological educators.[22]

4. Regarding curricula, Western theological educators would do well to encourage the introduction in former Soviet bloc evangelical institutions of:

a. courses on Eastern Orthodoxy and Catholicism which delineate common ground and insurmountable differences;[23] and

b. courses on biblical principles of conflict management. Unseemly strife abounds and demands serious attention within and between congregations, within and between denominations, within and between Christian confessions, and between Christians and persons of other faiths and no faith. Western Christian arbitration and conflict resolution services could be consulted for advice in developing instruction in this vital areas.[24]

5. Above all, Evangelical Christians, East and West, must foster and practice greater cooperation, especially in so expensive and labor intensive an endeavor as theological education.[25]

Author's Note:

The full title of the original article is "Theological Education After Communism: The Mixed Blessing of Western Assistance." Excerpts were reprinted in *East-West Church and Ministry Report* 3 Winter 1995): 11-12. The full text was published in Russian translation: "Bogoslovskoe obrazovanie v postkommunisticheskii period: polozhitel'nye i otritsatel'nye storony zapadnoi pomoshchi." *Put' bogopoznaniia*, No. 1 (1996): 17-25.

Notes

1. Mark Elliott, "Protestant Theological Education in the Former Soviet Union," *International Bulletin of Missionary Research* 18 (January 1994), 19.

2. Manfred Kohl, "Towards Globalization of Theological Education: Feasibility Study on Extending Theological Education into Eastern Europe and Parts of the Former USSR," thesis prospectus, Gordon-Conwell Theological Seminary, 15 October 1992, Appendix, 1.

3. Ralph H. Alexander, "Assessment of Leadership in Post-Communist Europe," Consultation on Theological Education and Leadership Development in Post-Communist Europe, Oradea, Romania, 5 October 1994, 3 and 5.

4. Walter Sawatsky, "Visions in Conflict: Starting Anew Through the Prism of Leadership Training Efforts" in *Religion after Communism in Eastern Europe*, Niels Nielsen, ed. (Boulder, CO: Westview Press 1994), 13 and 20.

5. Evro-Aziatskaya Akkreditatsionaya Assotsiatsiya," Protestanskoe dvizhenie v Rossii," 13-15, October 1994, conference brochure, 13-15.

6. R. Paul Stevens, "Marketing Faith—A Reflection on the Importing and Exporting of Western Theological Education," *Crux* 28 (June 1992), 12. See also Alexander, "Assessment of Leadership," 4. For an Adventist exception to the dependency cycle, see Elliott, "Protestant Theological Education," 16.

7. Kohl, "Towards Globalization," Appendix, 1.

8. Jack Graves, "Plugging the Theological Brain Drain," *Evangelical Missions Quarterly* 28 (April 1992), 153. See also "Bring Training in, Not People Out," Albanian Insight 20 (27 February 1992), p. 2.

9. Wilson Chow, "Theological Education: A Long and Hard Road," China Graduate School of Theology Bulletin (Winter 1993-94), 2.

10. For the globalization emphasis see various theme issues on this subject in *Theological Education* (Spring and Autumn 1986; Spring and Autumn 1993; Autumn 1993 Supplement); and Max L. Stackhouse, Apologia: Contextualization, Globalization, and Mission in *Theological Education* (Grand Rapids, MI: Eerdmans, 1988). For a brief overview see Robert J. Schreiter, "The ATS Globalization and Theological Education Project: Contextualization from a World Perspective," *Theological Education* 30 (Spring 1994), 81-88.

11. Alexander, "Assessment of Leadership," 2.

12. W. David Buschart, Kelvin G. Friebel, and Robert L. Webb, "Faith and Horizons: Biblical and Theological Studies in Non-Western Contexts" (Regina, Saskatchewan: Canadian Theological Seminary for the Association of Theological Schools, 1993), 5-6; Elliott, "Protestant Theological Education," 20.

13. Peter Kuzmic, "Vision for Theological Education for Difficult Times," Theological Education Conference, Moscow, Russia, 12 February 1993, 5.

14. Stevens, "Marketing Faith," 8.

15. Sawatsky, "Visions in Conflict," 19.

16. Author's notes, 5 February 1992.

17. The Western mainline Protestant rendering of the dilemma and its cure reads as follows: In contrast to professionally trained clergy, laity in the West have remained at a "literalist, elementary school level in their religious understanding," which can only be corrected by means of a "rigorous educational process and post-Enlightenment tools of analysis and interpretation (historical, literary, social, psychological, philosophical)." Edward Farley, *The Fragility of Knowledge, Theological Education in the Church & the University* (Philadelphia: Fortress Press, 1988), 92 and 99. Evangelicals in the former Soviet Union and East Central Europe, who will regard such medicine as worse than the ailment, must ask themselves what they really want from the West. Paradoxically, the East could subject itself to Western mainstream theological education's childlike faith in the sanctity of objective analysis just when Western intellectuals increasingly debunk the possibility of detached empiricism.

18. Stevens, "Marketing Faith," 8 and 11. In 1983 Edward Farley (*Theologia: The Fragmentation and Unity of Theological Education* [Philadelphia: Fortress Press, 1983], 19 and 22) bemoaned the fragmentation of Western theological education, setting off what David Kelsey has described as "the most extensive debate in print about theological schooling that has ever been published" (*Between Athens and Berlin; The Theological Education Debate* [Grand Rapids, MI: Eerdmans, 1993], 1). Torn between intellectual formation ("Berlin") and character and spiritual formation ("Athens"), between academic and professional preparation, between the theoretical and the practical, between head and heart, theological educators widely regard the lack of coherence in their enterprise as a given. (David H. Kelsey, *To Understand God Truly; What's Theological About a Theological School* [Louisville: Westminster/John Knox Press, 1992], 26, 105, and 232-33.) That the discussants in the debate have been predominately white male theological faculty in North American mainline Protestant schools (Kelsey, *Between Athens and Berlin*, 2) has led to additional fissures along lines of gender and color. See *The Mud Flower Collective, God's Fierce Whimsy: Feminism and Theological Education* (New York: Pilgrim Press, 1985).

19. Stevens, "Marketing Faith," 7-8.

20. Sawatsky, "Visions in Conflict," 12.

21. Points a. through d. are abridged versions of comments in Elliott, "Protestant Theological Education," 16.

22. "Introducing SAIACS." Contact: Dr. Graham Houghton, Principal, SAIACS, Box 7747, Kothanur P. O., Bangalore – 560077 India: tel: 0091-80-8465235; fax: 0091-80-5565547. The Norwegian Mission to the East is supporting seminarians from former Soviet bloc countries in India and the Philippines.

23. Sawatsky, "Visions in Conflict," 21-22.

24. Western centers whose work in post-Soviet societies could be invaluable include the Mennonite Central Committee, Box 500, Akron, PA 17501, and the Institute for Christian Conciliation, 1537 Avenue D. Suite 352, Billings, MT 59102.

25. Kuzmic, *Between Athens and Berlin*, 10-11; Alexander, "Assessment of Leadership," 3. Perhaps the most successful cooperative effort to date to assist leadership training has been a Russian theological text project jointly administered by Overseas Council for Theological Education and Missions and Peter Deyneka Russian Ministries. By the end of 1994 it is projected that 400,000 volumes will have been published for some 7,000 residential and extension course students in the former Soviet Union. Jack Graves, "Former Soviet Union Theological Infrastructure Project, Textbook Development Component" (Greenwood IN: Overseas Council for Theological Education and Missions, 1994).

Chapter 5

Pastoral Training Under Fire: A Review of Wayne Kenney, " 'A Conspiracy of Learning': Self-Directed Learning Among Protestant Russian Clergy Before 1987" (1997)

Although the title suggests a more comprehensive examination of the subject than the survey sample will allow, informative findings, nevertheless, make "A Conspiracy of Learning" noteworthy. The author used open-ended, life-story interviews with 13 pastors as the primary source for his research. Unfortunately, individuals chosen for the study represent a quite narrow portion of the Russian Protestant experience: 13 men from Moscow, mostly unregistered Baptist backgrounds, mostly between the ages of 25 and 44 (11 of 13), who in 1994 were participants in systematic but nonresidential ministry training programs. As a result, findings might or might not apply to the majority of Protestant pastors in the former Soviet Union who are non-Muscovites and non-Russians, and who represent registered Baptist, Pentecostal, and Lutheran denominations.

All interview subjects were highly motivated, eager learners. By definition, they placed a high value on education, as evidenced by their enrollment in Biblical Education by Extension (BEE) training courses. Nearly all were sons of pastors who had suffered harassment and imprisonment

---

Reprinted with permission from: *East-West Church & Ministry Report* 5 (Winter 1997): 13. Review of Ed.D. thesis, Pennsylvania State University, 1995, 220 pp.

under the Communists. Almost all (12 of 13) were married, with 3 to 11 children. Most had the equivalent of a tenth or eleventh grade education. And most held secular employment in addition to their pastoral duties.

Perhaps the terminology "self-directed learning" excluded evaluation of the hundreds of pastors who completed clandestine, then later legal, Evangelical Christian-Baptist correspondence courses, or the hundreds of Pentecostals who quietly managed informal correspondence courses provided by the Brussels-based Assemblies of God International Correspondence Institute. In any case, a closer evaluation of these programs, using Kenney's techniques, would document an experience that made a substantial contribution to the survival of Evangelical faith despite a hostile Soviet environment. In passing, it should be noted that Walter Sawatsky of Associated Mennonite Theological Seminary, Elkhart, IN, currently is helping coordinate a wide-ranging interview project to document the twentieth-century Evangelical experience in the Soviet Union.

Perhaps the most striking finding of Kenney's study is the degree to which the church leaders of those interviewed resisted the self-directed learning of young, aspiring ministers. While some of this opposition, no doubt, stemmed from an anti-intellectual bias exacerbated by a Communist ban on Evangelicals in higher education, the larger factor appears to have been the issue of control. Overwhelming authority in the hands of a pulpit autocrat is an oft-noted phenomenon in Soviet and post-Soviet Evangelical circles. One evidence of this phenomenon has been the attempt by church leaders to keep a close rein on all church activities. More than a few leaders have been inclined to prohibit study or outreach that could not be readily and completely directed from the top. The mostly younger pastors interviewed by Kenney expressed frustration, disappointment, and dismay at their superiors' heavy-handed efforts to thwart independent initiatives, from street preaching to informal theological study. In their defense, one huge extenuating circumstance loomed large for senior pastors prior to *glasnost*: state threats against their churches and their personal liberty should they not be able to "administer" their own flock in an "orderly" manner (read no new initiatives).

While Kenney's work is long on informal learning theory and a bit thin on the Russian Evangelical context, he does make a strong case that most literature on self-directed learning does not take into account non-

North American contexts where state intervention and cavalier treatment of civil liberties distort all of life, including the educational process. One would hope that Kenney's methodologies could be used to help determine strengths and weaknesses of the various current efforts to provide theological education to pastors in post-Soviet societies, including correspondence, extension, and formal residential programs.

Chapter 6
Recent Research on Evangelical Theological Education in Post-Soviet Societies (1999)

Two recent doctoral dissertations directly address the issue of Evangelical theological education in post-Soviet societies:

1. Charter, Miriam L. "Theological Education for New Protestant Churches of Russia: Indigenous Judgments on the Appropriateness of Educational Methods and Styles," Ph.D., Trinity Evangelical Divinity School, 1997; and

2. Bohn, David P. "The Perspectives on Theological Education Evident Among Evangelical Church Leaders in Bulgaria, Hungary, Romania and Russia," Ph.D., Trinity International University, 1997.

Similarities

Both dissertations were completed in 1997 at Trinity Evangelical Divinity School, now known as Trinity International University, Deerfield, IL, near Chicago. Dr. Ted Ward, a specialist in nonformal education, served as director for both theses. The authors, Miriam Charter and David Bohn both have extensive experience in the region, particularly East Central Europe, and both have worked for Biblical Education by Extension (BEE).

The present article is a revised version of a paper delivered at the Second Consultation on Theological Education and Leadership Development in Post-Communist Europe, Osijek, Croatia, 2 September 1998. Reprinted with permission from: *Religion in Eastern Europe* 19 (February 1999): 29-52.

Miriam Charter served with BEE from 1985 to 1992, primarily in Romania and Bulgaria, with more limited assignments in Czechoslovakia, Hungary, and Poland. She was a missionary with the Christian and Missionary Alliance in Krasnodar, Russia, 1995-96, and currently is director of adult education at First Alliance Church, Calgary, Alberta. David Bohn, who lives near Vienna, Austria, has worked for BEE since 1983, with a particular focus on leadership training in Romania.[1]

Both dissertations rest squarely on findings derived from survey research: ethnographic interviews in Dr. Charter's thesis, and questionnaire responses and interviews in Dr. Bohn's thesis. Both draw heavily upon indigenous perspectives, but Dr. Charter does include Western respondents. In 1995-96 Miriam Charter interviewed 66 students and 20 faculty at three institutions of "new" Protestants: two Russian (St. Petersburg Christian University and Lampados Bible College) and one Ukrainian (Donetsk Christian University). In 1996-97 David Bohn administered 12-page questionnaires to, and conducted interviews with, 36 denominational and seminary leaders and influential pastors from five denominations (Baptist, Brethren, Congregational, Pentecostal, and Reformed) from four nations (Hungary, Bulgaria, Romania, and Russia).

Given their BEE experience and the tutelage of nonformal advocate Dr. Ted Ward, it is not surprising that both see significant shortcomings in residential programs, favoring instead various alternatives to traditional degrees. What is surprising is the decision of both authors not to investigate nonformal efforts, such as BEE and the Pentecostal ICI University.[2] In their defense, both might argue that nonformal programs are, for them, known quantities, whereas post-Soviet residential seminary education is undergoing rapid expansion and evolution and deserves closer scrutiny. In any case, authors have every right to set the limits of their own investigations. But I personally wish, for the sake of comprehensive coverage, that Miriam Charter had chosen to include a Pentecostal institution in her study of "new" Protestant institutions, and that David Bohn had included Ukraine in his study because of the continuing, dynamic growth of all churches in what William Fletcher once called the Soviet "Bible Belt."

Contrasts

In addition to their common ground, the two studies evidence significant contrasts in coverage:

1. In terms of **geography**: both researched Russia, but only Miriam Charter investigated a Ukrainian institution, while only David Bohn included Hungary, Bulgaria, and Romania;

2. In terms of **denominations**: Miriam Charter examined exclusively institutions founded by "new" Protestants, churches legally recognized apart from the Soviet-sanctioned Evangelical Christian-Baptist Union since the 1960s (autonomous Baptists and Mennonites) or since the 1990s (Christian Missionary Union); in contrast, David Bohn researched exclusively schools founded by what are described as "historic denominations" which existed prior to the collapse of the Iron Curtain in 1989;

3. In terms of **respondents**: Miriam Charter interviewed predominantly students, while David Bohn interviewed exclusively leaders of denominations, seminaries, and prominent churches.

Making Generalizations Cautiously

Before exploring the wealth of findings in these thought-provoking studies, let me caution, as I am sure the authors would, that any generalizations drawn from their work, for the whole enterprise of post-Soviet Protestant theological education, require careful handling. Miriam Charter, in looking at three schools in Russia and Ukraine cannot speak directly of the other 13 former Soviet republics or East Central Europe, and she does not speak directly of the experience of the largest categories of schools: Evangelical Christian-Baptist, Pentecostal, and Charismatic. Similarly, David Bohn does not speak directly of experience outside Hungary, Bulgaria, Romania, and Russia. And despite their recent fieldwork, neither can be expected to be reporting today's circumstances. In fact, the dizzying pace of change often makes even last year's statistics and curriculum outdated. Still, Miriam Charter and David Bohn have given us a great deal of food for thought which can contribute to productive evaluation and reevaluation of every training program in the region.

Relating to The West

In attempting to summarize and critique the massive amount of material in these two pathbreaking works, I will organize my comments around the theme, "relating to the West." In broad strokes, let us keep in mind that East Central Europe and the Russian and Soviet empires have always assumed the West as the natural basis of comparison. The West has been hated and loved, but the frame of reference historically has always been the West, not the adjacent Near East, nor the Far East. Russians, for example, learned from Marx to despise Western capitalism, but Marxism itself is, as well, a Western construct. The nineteenth century Westernizer–Slavophile controversy in Russia also illustrates typically conflicting views of the West, but again, the Western orientation of the dispute is unmistakable. Thus, Miriam Charter rightly sees Nicholas Danilevsky and his 1871 love-hate polemic, *Russia and Europe*, as a telling harbinger of the dynamics to be found in new post-Soviet Evangelical seminaries, full at once of both fascination and fear of all things Western (iv, 195, 206, 241).

The centrality – and the ambivalence – of the relationship with the West can be seen in the priorities set by the Eurasian Accrediting Association of Evangelical Schools in October 1997 at its formal founding meeting near Moscow:

1. develop the Accrediting Association [so that students can study in country, rather than depend upon *Western* education];

2. increase national faculty [in order to decrease dependence upon *Western* faculty];

3. develop Russian theological texts by Russians [lessening dependence upon translations of *Western* texts];

4. increase cooperation between schools and churches [because schools will not survive without church support as *Western* financial support decreases]; and

5. become self-supporting [because Western funding cannot last at present levels and it means *Western* control].[3]

In one way or another, all these goals are healthy; they all contribute to contextualization; and they all should be encouraged by Western Christians.[4]

The Mixed Blessing of Western Assistance

In preparing a paper for the 1994 Oradea Consultation on Theological Education and Leadership Development, the phrase "mixed blessing" came to my mind to describe Western assistance for post-Soviet seminaries.[5] Similarly, Miriam Charter (190, 243-44) and David Bohn (193- 96, 309) report countless examples of respondents being of two minds over Western involvement. On the one hand, those interviewed typically believe the development of theological education would be impossible, or nearly impossible, without outside funding and organizational experience, translated textbooks, and Western professors with their knowledge, experience, and modeling of reflective, critical thinking.[6] One of David Bohn's respondents bluntly contends, "Without foreign people involved, no school could exist" (193). Those interviewed express a wide range of reservations, even hostility, concerning Western influence upon church leadership training. Fears include foreign control, a brain drain of the brightest to the West, denominational fragmentation, theological pluralism and liberalism, and in the former Soviet Union specifically, a pronounced wariness of Calvinism (Charter, 190, 240; Bohn, 96-98, 191, 306, 308-09). On Western miscues David Bohn quotes Fuller Seminary professor Miroslav Volf who maintains that the task of theological education is "not to import Jesus, like some exotic article from a foreign land. We must proclaim Jesus and, in obedience to his message of salvation, discover the Croatian or Slovakian, Hungarian, or Serbian face of Jesus."[7]

Admission Policies

Of all the problems addressed by these two dissertations, perhaps the most troubling to me personally concerns frequently lax seminary admission policies, the immediate impact they have on the composition of the student body, and the long-term impact they have on post-graduation performance. In many schools, especially in the former Soviet Union, students are very young, often only in their teens. Miriam Charter reports that Lampados Bible College accepts applicants with as little as ten years of public schooling who have been believers as little as two years. "It was not unusual to meet students who had begun their theological education at sixteen years of age" (119). Since many established pastors, often with large families, find it difficult or impossible to study in residential programs, young people, who often are new Christians, and who often have very little church experience, fill the classrooms of many seminaries. Despite an admission process that administrators consider adequate, seminarians interviewed by Miriam Charter themselves admitted, "the right students are not being trained in the schools" (118-19). David Bohn, likewise, discovered "careless admission of students to formal programs" in Russia, Romania, and Hungary (135, 146-47).

One Russian attributed indiscriminate admission policies to Western pressure to produce results: "All of the Western organizations have hard plans: how many people they need to graduate in a year. Sometimes they even take people off the street. Sometimes these people have no roots in the churches" (178). At a theological education consultation near Kyiv in September 1996 speakers noted "pressure mounting to enlarge student bodies" at least partly to justify each school's existence in the eyes of Western benefactors.[8] In contrast, now that the demand for training that had built up over many decades is subsiding, competition for students has become so intense that some schools have closed. The number of Evangelical Christian-Baptist institutions in the former Soviet Union, for example, declined from 24 in 1996 to 17 today.[9]

One Russian pastor reported not writing a letter of recommendation for an unworthy young person in his church, but the applicant was admitted to a theological institute anyway (Bohn, 179). In the same vein, Miriam Charter suggests that an "apparent scarcity of worthy recruits" fuels "the resultant competition for students" and low admission standards (228). One Moscow church planter contends that sometimes women are admitted to seminary programs only because "not enough men apply."[10] It thus comes as no surprise that interviews frequently identified seminarians with "no burning commitment to ministry," "no goals and no purpose whatever in being here," "nothing better to do," and "no calling" (Charter, 119, 115; Bohn, 135). One Russian reported, "We have people who decide to go to the theological institute only because they want to get away from the army" (Bohn, 170). At the same time, the provision of student stipends, a European and Soviet pattern, may encourage applicants without a clear calling, not to mention exacerbating the degree of dependence upon the West (Bohn,

250).¹¹ Other problematic student motives include "the desire to achieve social position" (Bohn, 132) and seminary study "as a stepping stone to emigration or study abroad" (Charter, 116), or to a profession with a secure salary (Charter, 117). Only a few students cited church planting as a goal, and few aspired to the pastorate, compared to the large number dreaming of a teaching career (Charter 115, 117, 230, 237; Bohn, 31).

Low admission standards have meant that many seminaries must give serious attention to basic spiritual formation: seminary students "are not formed leaders needing education, but people who need a lot of attention paid to them because they are new Christians" (Charter, 120). "They are born again. They have a new spirit. But morally there are many questions. We have to teach very strenuously Christian morality" (Bohn, 170). Students themselves suggested to Miriam Charter that "the priority in theological education today should go to those already ministering in the church, those having a deep sense of calling to the church, leadership skills, and giftedness which the church has already affirmed" (229).

Some may assume, at least with Miriam Charter's study, that nonselective admissions in the seminaries of "new" Protestants does not apply to institutions of longstanding denominations. But Peter Konovalchik, president of the Russian Union of Evangelical Christians-Baptists (ECB), is disturbed, as well, by admission policies in his denomination's schools. This past October at a Eurasian Accrediting Association meeting, he raised, in forceful terms, many of the same reservations for ECB schools as those noted above:

> People (19 and 20 years old) go to seminaries who have not had a call of God, not those proven in their church service. Many have been members of churches only two or three years. Seminarians are separated from their churches and are not necessarily firm in the faith. Graduates have a problem: the church is not ready to receive them. Sixty percent do not become pastors because they are separated from their churches. What are we to do with graduates? Big money has been spent on them but they don't want to be pastors, but professors.
>
> I am convinced that a teacher needs to be a pastor first. We need education that is connected with practice. If a person has knowledge but cannot pass it on (how to preach), he has

nothing. We must stress homiletics. Each seminarian should at least lead a small group, but one rector told me they don't have time. A graduate does not even know how to lead a small group. Theory should not be separated from practice: This is the most important thing.[12]

Seminary–Church Relations

Rev. Konovalchik questions not only who is being educated, but he questions for what purpose. For many it would seem axiomatic that a major goal of seminary education would be to train church leadership; but Konovalchik identifies a seminary-church gap, some might even say chasm, that thwarts this aim. In addition to youthful inexperience and lack of calling already noted, the gap is widened in some instances by graduates who are full of theoretical knowledge and intellectual pride who balk at service in remote districts (Bohn, 133-34, 166-67; Charter, 120).

> Mature persons who have proven themselves in ministry are sent by their church to a theological school to be trained as teachers. In addition to a general theological education, each future teacher pursues a specialization in one discipline, with a view to returning to a two-fold task: (1) pastoring or planting a new church (in which they function as a *teaching pastor*) and (2) teaching in a local theological school as a resource in one discipline (234).

At the same time, Dr. Charter calls for a *"preaching faculty,"* that is, seminary teachers who at the same time "serve in local churches" (223). But to succeed, she cautions, this scheme, now being tested in Moldova, "must draw on a committed group of churches because of the increased number of faculty members it requires" (233-34).

What *is* the Purpose of Theological Education?

Where admission policies lack coherence and a seminary-church gap looms large, the absence of a clear seminary mission statement may be to blame. Miriam Charter rightly notes:

> Confusion exists as to what is the purpose of theological education in Russia today. Unfortunately, in some situations

it seems only to exist for itself. In others there are stated intentions of the equipping of a clerical elite. Those groups specifically attached to church planting movements believe their educational interventions will result in the development of pastors and church planters for new churches. In the midst of this ambivalence, the question remains: is the intended outcome one of critiquing the faith (the development of theologians and scholars), the preparing of mature Christians (spiritual development of leaders), or the practical training of pastors, church workers, and church planters (227)?

Between 1990 and 1997 in the former Soviet Union over 100 Protestant seminaries and Bible schools opened, and dozens more emerged or reemerged in East Central Europe.[13] Understanding the dynamics involved is no simple task. To be sure, the pent-up demand of many decades and the sudden collapse of communist proscriptions and restrictions in 1989-91 triggered an unprecedented wave of school openings. Unfortunately, energetic institution building evidenced more passion and enthusiasm than sober reflection on precisely what seminaries were to accomplish. From his respondents David Bohn concludes that confusion reigns "as to the primary task of theological education" (298). To clarify goals Miriam Charter has elaborated a series of fundamental questions that should prove helpful to everyone concerned (Western partners, seminary administrators, faculty, students, and churches).

1. Is the intended outcome, understood by the investing constituency, the same outcome the school administrators/students have in view?

2. Is the general constituency serviced by this institution already serviced by another school of similar type, within reasonable distance, thereby creating a competition for the same potential students?

3. What is the school's declared purpose? What are its entrance requirements for new students? Do the type of students recruited possess the qualities needed by the type of Christian worker the schools claim to produce?

4. What type/level of education is proposed? Is the type of education proposed by this school a duplication of services offered by

another, already existent school within reasonable distance, for which it would not theologically be a problem for students in churches to attend?

5. What are the school's relationships with indigenous groups in the country? Does the school play a role in the agenda of an indigenous group of churches or is it primarily fulfilling the vision of a Western mission/organization whose business is the establishing of educational systems around the world (239-40)?

A workshop in each institution, including each of the school's various constituencies, designed to identify and prioritize goals and expectations would not be a painless exercise, but it could be invaluable in building unity of purpose and in avoiding greater pain and even fatal divisions in the future. Theological education typically is the most expensive enterprise any Christian community ever undertakes. Trained faculty, instructional facilities, libraries, textbook development all take a great deal of time and money. Consequently, all concerned should be absolutely clear that they are of one mind as to the purpose or purposes of such an extraordinary effort.

Evaluating Theological Education by Outcomes

In the West today, the mantra in educational evaluation is the word *outcomes*. Accrediting bodies and specialists in pedagogy are expecting educational enterprises at all levels to identify their goals and to document the attainment of those goals through the lives of their graduates. Miriam Charter fairly represents this current evaluative tool as she writes, "Investors, educators, and church leaders must think more strategically about what the intended outcome of their investment is, what kind of student should be admitted to the schools, and what kind of faculty appointed so as to achieve those outcomes" (227; see also 225, 259-60). It seems reasonable that surveying alumni is a helpful and workable way to measure success, because expectations for graduates and the actual vocations of graduates can be readily compared.

This summer St. Petersburg Christian University (SPCU) faculty member Alexander Negrov shared with a group of East Europeans studying at Wheaton College the results of a survey of SPCU's first 111 graduates.

St. Petersburg Christian University Graduates

Vocation	Number	Percentage
Pastor	6	5.41
Work in Church	36	32.43
Missionary	12	10.81
Church Planter	8	7.21
Pursuing Advanced degree	9	8.11
Teaching in Bible College	14	12.61
Director of Bible College	3	2.70
Other (not following Christ, not attending church, or emigrated abroad	23	20.70
TOTAL	111	100%

SPCU is to be commended for taking this measure of its own success and making the results known. It is noteworthy that 79 percent of graduates are in full-time Christian service, or are receiving further training to that end. At the same time, that nearly a third are "working in churches" could be a troubling finding if it is the case that congregations will not accept these graduates as pastors. It also would be instructive to compare the vocations of male and female graduates.

Another potentially troubling point could be the comparison of 5.5 percent of graduates serving as pastors with 21 percent teaching or pursuing advanced degrees. If particular donors gave primarily to assist the training of local pastors, the above outcomes could raise questions. However, assuming the preparation of seminary teachers is a stated goal, St. Petersburg Christian University already has achieved solid results. In any case, SPCU deserves credit for taking such an objective step to evaluate the results of its educational program. Furthermore, I suspect its level of success will compare very favorably with many other institutions, once comparative data become available.[14]

Curriculum

A clear institutional mission statement should shape not only admission policies, but curriculum. We may or may not always agree with the priorities of those surveyed in these two dissertations, or even the conclusions drawn. But we all are indebted to Miriam Charter and David Bohn because of their careful attention to the perspectives of respondents. As noted earlier, Russians and Ukrainians interviewed by Miriam Charter made a strong case for careful mentoring of students who are young in age and young in faith. Schools would, of course, prefer to accept only applicants who are mature Christians, but candidates often lack that attribute. Thus, given current admission policies, seminaries must address "the developmental need of many young Christians" who "do not have thespiritual formation needed to become effective servants of the Gospel" (204; see also 191, 193, 216). To this end, in addition to faculty mentoring and counseling, seminaries may need to require courses in ethics and define community standards very clearly to combat widespread cheating, which David Bohn's respondents, among many others, have noted (93, 175, 177, 304).[15]

Respondents also desire a strong curricular emphasis upon theology to clarify doctrine and denominational distinctives and to combat cults (Bohn, 137).[16] In turn, sound theology must be communicated to believers, hence Miriam Charter's stress upon strong preaching (237).[17]

One respondent referred to in David Bohn's thesis speaks of the need to understand and relate to secular society (162). What Peter Kuzmic stressed on this point at Oradea in 1994 bears repeating: the absolute necessity of bridging "the Biblical world and the contemporary world," in other words, "the task of contextualization: of remaining faithful to the Biblical Gospel, open to the Holy Spirit, but also of being open to learning in a continual dialogue with our society." Kuzmic believes, therefore, that seminarians should study such subjects as psychology, philosophy, and sociology in order to be understood in the modern world. He would say the Gospel never changes, but the audience for it changes constantly. As German theologian Helmut Thielicke put it, "The Gospel must be constantly forwarded to a new address because the recipient is repeatedly changing his place of residence."[18]

To prepare seminarians to engage nonbelievers, another task of the curriculum should be to encourage analytical thinking. Miriam Charter correctly notes that Soviet pedagogy stressed memorization and the uncritical acceptance of received wisdom. In contrast, some Western educators, Americans in particular, stress the importance of teaching students "to engage in independent, reflective thinking." By this means, seminarians will more likely own their theology, rather than simply parrot it (243-44; see also 204, 214, 236). As Peter Penner of St. Petersburg Christian University has argued, graduates need "the ability to use knowledge independently in order to deal with concrete questions."[19]

One of David Bohn's respondents wrote that in the communist system, "There was the atheistic view of the world and the Christian view of the world, and there is nothing in between these two views. We never thought that believers could have different ideas on the same topic" (238). Some even yearn for the "good old days" of communism, perceived as having been more predictable, without the constant bombardment of mind-boggling choices. David Bohn reports a Bulgarian respondent's analogy, which many of us have heard repeatedly, that compares disoriented post-Soviet citizens to the Hebrew children who said they preferred the "security" of slavery in Egypt to the uncertainty of freedom in the Sinai (Bohn, 399-400). In contrast, one Romanian values Western teaching precisely because it encourages critical reflection and the ability "to evaluate and systematize information. My hope is that we will get information, we will get training, but even more I hope that we will be equipped how to select that which is good. There is a kind of maturity in rejecting some things and accepting others in theology" (Bohn, 197-98).

As noted, this question of choice, and what might be called discrimination in its positive sense, among ideas, rather than among people, is as likely to paralyze as to liberate people enduring communist withdrawal. Indeed, discernment, which the best theological education will cultivate, does not come easy. What David Bohn calls "choice overload" (185) threatens new seminaries as much as it threatens seminarians; foreigners offer a "cafeteria" (249) or a "smorgasbord" (198) of ideas and projects:

> After Communism fell, great numbers of mission agencies, churches, and individuals came offering many kinds of assistance. Nationals entered a state of choice shock. Opportunities that had taken decades to develop in the West were compressed, packaged, and offered. Initially almost all offers were accepted. Yet discretion is the better part of

choice, and eventually nationals began to find a way to be selective (198-99).

Just as seminarians benefit from the skill of critical analysis (all ideas are not equally good or bad), so seminary leaders benefit from the same skill as they evaluate offers of help (all Western partners and programs are not equally good or bad). As one Hungarian Pentecostal put it, "We need to learn how to select and not accept everyone without judging" (Bohn, 199; see also 278; and Charter, 133).

Pros and Cons of Non-formal Education

Both dissertations argue that the best choice that East European educators can make is not to adopt the traditional residential Western approach to theological education, at least not without very serious adaptation. Miriam Charter writes,

> The most redemptive role for Westerners in the inevitable partnership of East and West in the development of theological education must be one of encouragement intentionally encouraging educators not to allow the West, unchallenged, to replicate the educational models and styles that they have implemented in countries around the world (261).

Likewise, David Bohn equates reform in theological education with movement away from formal, residential programs and the implementation of one or another nonformal model. Slightly more than half of his respondents agreed with his survey item that stated, "Post-Communist countries are forfeiting a marvelous opportunity to initiate theological education reform" (120). As he envisions it, reform would involve a "multiple-step approach to ministry" proficiency involving "various educational experiences and 'street' competencies," an approach that has worked well in Latin America and Mexico (297-98). Despite respondents' stated support for reform, Dr. Bohn appears to be disappointed that, even though many have benefited directly from BEE, ECB, and other nonresidential programs, they "almost invariably [have] turned their focus to formal schooling, as if drawn by an irresistible force" (296)[20] Drs. Bohn and Charter regret this trend because they see nonformal education as closer to the church, more practical, and meeting the needs of those already engaged in ministry for whom formal schooling is not an option, not to mention much less expensive (Bohn, 142- 44; Charter, 218, 222). However, it should be pointed out that Alexander Romonyuk, head of BEE Ukraine, shared at a June 1998 conference that the full BEE program in the former Soviet Union now takes eight years to complete, that the dropout rate is high, and that graduates do not receive recognized degrees. In addition, nonresidential programs typically lack the regular student-to-student and student-faculty interaction of a residential community that can so enhance student spiritual and academic development.[21]

My own opinion is that theological education in communism's wake need not be cast in terms of formal versus nonformal. Both have their place and can be complimentary. Ukrainian Bible Training Center Association, which was founded by former BEE staff member Abraham Bible, and which uses BEE course materials, enrolled 6,921 students in spring 1998, with an additional 1,500 students enrolled in Russia. In addition, an array of other smaller denominational and parachurch programs provide nonresidential instruction.[22] The Pentecostal ICI University also supports numerous modular and church-based courses with hundreds of students. Especially for Russia and Ukraine, where distances are great and formal Protestant theological education is in its infancy, nonformal instruction will continue to be critically important for the foreseeable future. At the same time, strong, highly respected, accredited residential seminaries are fervently desired throughout East Central Europe and the former Soviet Union. They are the priority, and notwithstanding the pedagogical preferences of some Westerners to the contrary, residential programs likely will continue to receive the bulk of the educational funding and effort for the foreseeable future.

A Question of Respect

On various occasions I have been in conversations with advocates of nonformal education who have argued that Western influence is responsible for the East European passion for formal programs. However, I would contend that, without any Western coaxing, post-Soviet Protestants desperately desire academically strong residential seminaries as one means of overcoming the perception that they are second class citizens and culturally marginal. David Bohn has his reservations, but he does report that his "respondents consistently think that an accredited degree increases the respect of society for evangelicals" (258).

Because of illness in my family I was not able to deliver in person my paper on the mixed blessing of Western assistance to theological education at the Oradea Conference in 1994. But from those in attendance I gather that many East Europeans were not convinced by various presentations warning of the shortcomings of accredited degree programs, as often as not, delivered paradoxically by persons with earned doctorates. From the perspective of 1998 I understand the East European position much better than I did. If among the tasks of theological education we Evangelicals have in mind to engage and transform society, we must understand society and have the communication and homiletic skills, as well as the knowledge, necessary to command public attention. This is a sophisticated and demanding assignment that I personally believe a resident community of faculty and students can better address than can the best nonformal program.

East European Evangelicals desire traditional accredited institutions to escape the sense of still being "outlaws," to gain a "sense of legitimacy," and "to shift the balance of power which now favors the Orthodox church" (Bohn, 253, 324). One Russian Baptist pastor declared he would not "waste his time" in an unaccredited institution: "An official degree is very important because if you don't have an official degree, you don't have any weight, you don't mean anything to anybody" (Bohn, 258).

Miriam Charter, who finds such an argument unconvincing, counters with the Russian faculty member who regrets "schools [that] succumb to the pressure from the West to raise academic levels, publish books, and aspire to Western accreditation standards, the practical motivation to prepare people for Christian ministry is overshadowed by the pressure to simulate Western academic standards" (121-22). David Bohn, who is as skeptical as Miriam Charter is of the emphasis upon formal academic training, approvingly quotes nonformal advocate Michael Griffiths[23] who calls "the desire for evangelical scholarship" an "insidious blight" and "virus" (35-36), and Regent College professor Paul Stevens, who equates it with an unbecoming "pride in degrees and publishing" (34; see also 65, 300).

Unquestionably, formal and nonformal programs and academic and practical emphases have their advantages and disadvantages. Often it is a question of balance. For example, academic rigor and recognized credentials can be a means of impacting society, but they also can contribute to unChristlike vainglory. For Christian educators the promise and peril of learning are best kept in a healthy tension. As regards the place of intellect in Christian experience and in theological education, I like what seventeenth century Christian apologist and scientist Blaise Pascal concluded: "Two mistakes: to exclude reason, and to admit no argument but reason."[24]

Accreditation Requirements and Western Dependence

Everyone seems to agree that long-term dependence upon the West is not healthy for theological education in the East. Be that as it may, the consensus among East European educators in favor of strong academics, degree programs, and accreditation is bound to prolong and deepen dependency – *if* the West sustains the will to pay. Simply put, accrediting standards for facilities, trained faculty, and libraries, and equally essential textbook development, require tremendous financial investments, and, at present, only Western partners, and only some of them, have that kind of money.[25]

At the first post-Soviet interdenominational gathering of Protestant theological educators in Moscow in February 1993, the need for textbooks was the most frequently voiced concern. In response, Overseas Council for Theological Education and Peter Deyneka Russian Ministries partnered to identify, locate, and print or reprint relevant titles for use in seminaries. This Bible Pulpit Series has made an invaluable contribution to the development of Protestant theological education in Russia. In the next phase of assistance, all parties concerned (donors, administrators, faculty, and students) recognize the need to encourage indigenous authors. Miriam Charter noted, "The urgency of developing indigenous writers in theology was voiced by nearly every respondent. One student remarked that the Orthodox Church views Protestants as a sect because 'We don't even have a theological text of our own. They don't even want to argue with us'" (134; see also 125, 127, 132-36; Bohn, 106, 234-36).

Many new seminary libraries have relatively large English collections; many of the holdings in the mother tongue do not relate to theological education; and in traditionally Orthodox countries, Orthodox writers sometimes outnumber Protestant authors in the stacks. Miriam Charter reported, "It was not unusual to find a student who had an acceptable command of English, sitting in the library, surrounded by her classmates, translating for them, sentence by sentence, an English textbook required for a class (123).²⁶

Because of the heavy dependence upon Western professors and English texts, or texts translated from English, some respondents fear the emergence of an anglicized Slavic Protestant faith: "A journalist came to my church recently. She commented that she had heard many English expressions in the [Russian] sermon not rich as it might have been, had it been delivered in good Russian" (Charter, 127). As a corrective, Dr. Charter makes a valuable recommendation to have schools offer "courses which have as a goal the writing of significant, biblically rich, contextualized books" in the indigenous language (238), although such offerings might best be reserved for advanced students.

Russian Bible school graduate and church planter Valeri Pryamilov, like many in Eastern Europe, believes the greatest need in theological education today — even more important than books — is well-trained indigenous faculty.²⁷ In light of accreditation requirements and the mixed blessing of Western assistance, no need appears to be more pressing — and more problematic — than faculty development. The conundrum in the post-Soviet era is that contextualized theological education requires trained indigenous faculty. But obtaining the necessary degrees, almost without exception, involves Westernization. If faculty who complete higher degrees abroad repatriate — by no means a safe assumption — they and their families invariably face traumatic economic and cultural readjustment back home.²⁸ Other drawbacks to study abroad include the transmission of Western theological controversies from West to East and the cultural irrelevance of much of Western theological instruction for the post-Soviet context.

Dr. Graham Houghton, principal of India's South Asia Institute of Advanced Christian Studies, in his Institute's information brochure pointedly highlights three rationales for doctoral training in country: the brain drain via study abroad; cost effectiveness of study in country; and the "considerable lack of relevance about much that is studied in Western countries."²⁹ David Bohn's respondents commented on the dangers of study abroad at length and with considerable feeling. A seminary educator from Bulgaria stated, "My greatest hope is that people who are in the West will come back. I hope that those who return will not bring false or liberal teaching, or extreme desires" (168). And a Romanian pastor laments, "I must say I have seen very,

very few situations where those who have been to the West have come back better. They put a lot of knowledge in their head. But when they come back, unfortunately, they have lost the power" (193; see also 95-97, 166, 168, 229-30, 306, 316-17; Charter, 116-17, 194, 241).[30]

Russian Evangelical Christian-Baptist leader Peter Konovalchik put it frankly, "A new convert went to England to study four years; he came back with new teaching that we don't want." Similarly, Moscow itself poses the threat of a brain drain for the rest of Russia. The majority of students in one Moscow Bible college are not from the capital and less than half of its graduates have returned to their homes. Some find jobs with Western missions, even as drivers, to avoid leaving the relatively easier life there. A Siberian Baptist asked Rev. Konovalchik, "Why should we send a student to Moscow? He won't return."[31]

A very few select students who are especially capable and dedicated probably should study abroad in order ultimately to strengthen programs at home. Hopefully, then, larger numbers will not need to study abroad and be tempted by the lure of the West.[32] In two previous articles I suggested various means of minimizing Western residence.[33] In the same vein, David Bohn makes the sensible recommendation that programs be developed that involve "a rhythm of study abroad and ministry at home" (232).[34] In 1994 I also suggested that India might be considered as a location for doctoral study. Solidly Evangelical institutions there could train doctoral candidates from the former Soviet Union and East Central Europe at a fraction of the cost of a Western education. OMS International intends for selected Russian students to do doctoral work at South Asia Institute of Advanced Christian Studies (SAIACS), in Bangalore, India, which employs eight PhDs and offers fully accredited doctor of philosophy and doctor of missiology degrees. Also, Russian and Ukrainian Pentecostals plan to train their advanced students at the M.A. level at Southern Asia Bible College, an Assemblies of God institution, also in Bangalore, India, and also with a substantial number of faculty with earned doctorates. Both schools are accredited by the Asia Theological Association. It would appear to be a reasonable assumption that students studying in Bangalore will be less tempted to remain abroad than those studying, for example, in Boston.[35] David Bohn notes that Bong Rin Ro, executive secretary of the Asia Theological Association, is another voice recommending theological education closer to home (61-62, 316).

The Prospect for Higher Degrees in Country

Ideally, in the future, seminary faculty will be able to obtain advanced degrees in country, without having to study abroad. Building the necessary doctoral programs, however, will be so costly and so labor-intensive that interdenominational cooperation would seem to be imperative. Unfortunately, despite affirmations of the need for joint efforts, "when the practical suggestion is made to have only one or two cooperative, advanced-degree institutions in each country," East European educators agree, but denominational leaders and influential pastors do not (Bohn, 107, 315-16; see also187, 286, 317). "Until these two groups of opinion leaders see the need for cooperative efforts to provide quality education for higher degrees," David Bohn probably is correct in concluding, "it seems unlikely that initiatives in this direction will succeed" (316). What is worse, insufficient interdenominational cooperation actually is compounded by increased Western denominational and parachurch support: "Denominations do not have a strong incentive to cooperate when each is able to cultivate its own sources of outside support" (Bohn, 310).[36]

Conclusion

Discussions of *advanced* degrees and *quality* education always make me nervous. Why? Because they have to do not just with gaining knowledge, but with gaining respect. For Christian educators—indeed, for all Christians the question has to be asked: how important should it be to gain respect? And from whom should we seek respect? As noted earlier, we can be pleased when seminary graduates with accredited degrees have honed the skills that will provide them an entree with the unchurched. At the same time, it has to be acknowledged that a perverse pride all too frequently accompanies learning. Only sore knees from much prayer can save a seminary graduate, and even more so a seminary professor with a new Ph.D., from insufferable arrogance. For Christians in general, and for Christians in higher education in particular, there is a constant need to balance biblical teaching on the depravity and the dignity of humankind. Jeremiah (17:9) reminds us that "the heart is deceitful above all things and beyond cure." And our apparent cosmic insignificance is underscored by David in Psalm 8:3-4: "When I consider your heavens, the work of your fingers, the moon and the stars, which you have set in place, what is man that you are mindful of him, the son of man that you care for him?" Yet in one of the most profound paradoxes of Scripture, the same psalm boldly affirms that God has deigned to invest in us a status just below His own, "crowned with glory and honor," and has made us ruler over all His creation (Psalm 8:5-8). My point is this: We have to constantly check our motives in all humility before the Lord as we strive for respect. Do we want it so that the Lord might be honored or so that we might be treated with greater deference? Or are noble and ignoble motives intertwined?

On various occasions in my years on the faculty at Wheaton College I have heard colleagues ponder what it would take for Wheaton to command the respect of the University of Chicago. Personally, this *respected* university is so thoroughly secularized that I would fear the day it would take Wheaton College seriously, because I would fear it would mean that Wheaton by that point had squandered its spiritual inheritance for a mess of porridge. I mention Wheaton only to illustrate that striving for respect is a predictable feature of higher education, including Christian, and that it will not end with accreditation. East European educators must anticipate that the pursuit of respect can be healthy or unhealthy, but in any case it will be unending. And whatever the advantages or disadvantages of becoming respected in the eyes of other institutions, accrediting bodies, secular society, or the West, we need constantly to remind ourselves that, as Paul writes, ultimately, we "study to show ourselves approved unto God" (II Timothy 2:15).

Notes

1. Contact information is as follows: Dr. Miriam Charter, 7375 4A Street SW, #509, Calgary, Alberta T2V 4Y8 Canada; tel: (403) 640-1289; e-mail: 74724.2255@compuserve.com; Dr. David Bohn, Muehlengasse 20, A-3400 Klosterneuberg, Austria; tel: 43-2243-25-218; e-mail: 71431.403@compuserve.com.

2. ICI formerly stood for International Correspondence Institute. For an examination of the experience of unregistered Russian Baptist pastors enrolled in BEE courses, see Wayne Kenney, " 'A Conspiracy of Learning': Self-Directed Learning Among Protestant Russian Clergy Before 1987," Ed.D. dissertation, Pennsylvania State University, 1995. A review appears in the East-West Church and Ministry Report 5 (Winter 1997), 13.

3. Peter Mitskevich, "Christian Education in Eurasia," Eurasia Symposium '98, First Baptist Church, Dallas, TX, 19-21 February 1998, 11-12.

4. Three of the four curricular priorities of Russians interviewed by Miriam Charter involved contextualization: the development of indigenous theology, indigenous preaching, indigenous writers, and pedagogical skills (235).

5. See the Appendix for a listing of interdenominational meetings on post-Soviet theological education. Mark Elliott, "Theological Education After Communism: The Mixed Blessing of Western Assistance," *Asbury Theological Journal* 50 (Spring 1995), 67. For a Russian reprint, see: "Bogoslovskoe obrazovanie v postkommunisticheskii period: polozhitel'nye i otritsatel'nye storony zapadnoi pomoshchi," *Put' bogopoznaniia*, no. 1 (1996): 17-25. Papers from the Oradea conference and papers written in response to it will be published in a forthcoming volume edited by Peter Kuzmic: *Equipping for the Future: Theological Education and Leadership Development in Post-Communist Europe*.

6. See also Igor K., "Difficulties and Prospects at the Lutheran Theological Seminary [Bratislava, Slovakia]," *The Zion* 73 [November-December 1997], 11-13.

7. See also Peter Kuzmic, "A Vision for Theological Education for Difficult Times," *Religion, State and Society* 22 (June 1994), 239.

8. Mark Elliott, "Post-Soviet Protestant Theological Education: Come of Age?" *Asbury Theological Journal* 53 (Fall 1998), forthcoming.

9. Comment of Vladimir Ryaguzov, director, Evangelical Christian-Baptist Correspondence Institute, at the Conference on Alternative Theological Education, St. Petersburg, Russia, 16 June 1998. The author wishes to thank Matt Miller, Moscow-based Evangelical Free Church missionary, for sharing notes and documents from this meeting. On the fragility of many of the new private institutions of higher education in East Central Europe see Hans C. Giesecke, "The Rise of Private Higher

Education in East Central Europe," unpublished paper, 6. See also Bohn, 47; 243; Charter, 121; Kuzmic, "Vision," 243.

10. Author's interview with Valeri Pryamilov, Center for Evangelism, Moscow, 17 July 1998.

11. *Ibid.*

12. Author's notes from Eurasian Accrediting Association meeting near Moscow, 13 October 1997.

13. Alla Tikhonova, Association for Spiritual Renewal, Moscow, has compiled several editions of a directory of seminaries in the former Soviet Union. For a review of Protestant leadership training in tsarist, Soviet, and the early post-Soviet periods see Mark Elliott, "Protestant Theological Education in the Former Soviet Union," *International Bulletin of Missionary Research* 18 (January 1994), 14-22.

14. Donetsk Christian University (DCU) graduated 366 students between 1991 and 1998. Seventy-five percent are in full-time Christian service; twenty percent "are involved in lay ministry in their local churches;" and the whereabouts of five percent of graduates is unknown. E-mail from Professor Ray Prigodich, Denver Seminary, sharing data from Aleksei Melnichuk, DCU, 19 August 1998.

15. Steven R. Chapman, "Collectivism in the Russian World View and Its Implications for Christian Ministry," *East-West Church & Ministry Report* 6 (Fall 1998), 13; Tom Hundley, "Poland Tolerates the Art of Academic Cheating," *Chicago Tribune*, 6 December 1998, Section 1, p. 2.

16. See also Mitskevich, "Christian Education," 9.

17. Rev. Konovalchik made the same case for homiletics in the October 1997 Moscow meeting.

18. Kuzmic, "Vision," 242.

19. Peter Penner, "Theologische Ausbildung—Eine Verpflichtende Mission: Faktoren zur Bestimmung von Leitlinien für Theologische Ausbildung in der GUS [Theological Education—An Engaging Mission: Factors for Defining Guidelines for Theological Education in the CIS]," Ph.D. dissertation, University of South Africa, 1998, Section 4.1.2.

20. David Bohn notes that all the Romanian church leaders questioned "had significant exposure to the extension model," but argues that extension education did not "touch in a significant way" Russian respondents who became leaders after the fall of communism (290). Granted, far more Romanian than Russian leaders had BEE courses, but I believe many, if not all, current Russian church leaders have had experience with some denominational extension programs.

21. Comments of Alexander Romonyuk, BEE Ukraine, and Johannes Lange, academic dean, St. Petersburg Christian University Conference on Alternative Theological Education, St. Petersburg, 16-18 June 1998.

22. Alexander Romonyuk, Conference on Alternative Theological Education, 16-18 June 1998; Richard Walsman, UBTCA, phone conversation with Sharyl Corrado, 8 December 1998. For a case study of the ongoing development of one nonresidential program, see Hannes Furter and Michael Huggins, "Grass-Root TEE Development in Russia and Central Asia," *TEE Journal*, forthcoming.

23. David Bohn cites Henry Griffith, but the actual source of the quotes is his bibliography reference for Michael Griffiths.

24. Blaise Pascal, *The Essential Pascal* (New York: New American Library, 1996), 200.

25. Sergei Sannikov, speaking for the Eurasian Accrediting Association in June 1998 at the St. Petersburg Alternative Theological Education Conference, stated that standards for evaluating programs would not be based on graduates, but on various aspects of the "academic process," such as "hours in class, testing methods, pages read, organizational stability, organizational legality, office management, program leadership and administration, [and] student activities." On the need for and the difficulty of realizing selfsufficiency, see also Penner, "Theologische Ausbildung," Section 4.4.3.

26. Some East Europeans recommend a command of English for seminarians because of the wealth and diversity of theological literature in that language (Bohn, 240).

27. Author's interview with Valeri Pryamilov, 17 July 1998.

28. A Western denominational missions administrator who wishes to remain anonymous shared with the Institute for East-West Christian Studies in August 1998 that 85 percent of the seminarians from the former Soviet Union funded by his church for study in the West have not returned home. This "bright flight," sadly, is not surprising, judging from earlier rates of non-return for other countries, which are comparable. See Elliott, "Mixed Blessing," 69; and Jack Graves, "Plugging the Theological Brain Drain," *Evangelical Missions Quarterly* 28 (April 1992), 155.

29. *Introducing SAIACS*.

30. See also Danut Manastireanu, "Evangelical Denominations in Post-Communist Romania," *East-West Church & Ministry Report* 6 (Spring 1998), 2.

31. Author's notes from meeting near Moscow, 13 October 1997; author's interview with Valeri Pryamilov, 17 July 1998.

32. See Wally C. Schoon, "The Lure of the West," *East-West Church and Ministry Report* 4 (Spring 1996), 1-2.

33. Elliott, "Protestant Theological Education," 16; and Elliott, "Mixed Blessing," 71.

34. Russians studying at Concordia Theological Seminary (Lutheran Church Missouri Synod), Ft. Wayne, IN, return home for a full year's ministerial practicum between their first and third year of study in the West. This has reduced the problem of brain drain, "although some admit that it is hard to go back." Sharyl Corrado's notes based on a phone conversation with Jan Pillsbury, 5 October 1998.

35. Author's conversation with Dr. J. B. Crouse, president, OMS International, 23 May 1998; author's phone conversation with Rev. Jerry Parsley, field director for Eurasia, Division of Foreign Missions, Assemblies of God, Springfield, MO, 27 August 1998; John Higgins to Sharyl Corrado, 27 August 1998. Contact information for the schools follows: Dr. Graham Houghton, Principal, SAIACS, Box 7747, Kothanur, Bangalore 560 077, India; tel: 91-80-846-5235; fax: 91-80-846-5412; e-mail: saiacs@giasbg01.vsnl.net.in; website: http://www.epinay.com/saiacs; Dr. Ivan Satyavrata, Principal, Southern Asia Bible College, Kothanur, Bangalore 560 077, India; tel: 91-80-546-8651; fax: 91-80-557-5541.

36. In fact, in some cases, cooperation in theological education has declined in the post-communist era: David Bohn (10-11) notes the demise of a Protestant interdenominational seminary sponsored by the Council of Free Churches in Hungary, and the same can be said of a joint Protestant effort in Poland.

Appendix

Interdenominational Meetings on Post-Soviet Theological Education

Date	Location	Title	Sponsors/Hosts	Number Attending
3 Sept. 1992	Wheaton, IL	A Consultation on Theological Education in the Former Soviet Union	Overseas Council for Theological Education; Peter Deyneka Russian Ministries; Institute for East-West Christian Studies	17 Westerners
11 February 1993	Moscow, Russia	Christian Leadership Training and Theological Conference (Conference on Theological Education in the Former Soviet Union)	Overseas Council; Peter Deyneka Russian Ministries; Institute for East-West Christian Studies	75, including 38 Westerners
16 April 1993	Wheaton, IL	Christian Higher Education in the Former Soviet Union: A Consultation	Institute for East-West Christian Studies	66, mostly Westerners
4-8 Oct. 1994	Oradea, Romania	Equipping for the Future: Consultation on Theological Education and Leadership Development in the Post-Communist World	Overseas Council	94, including 44 Westerners

Date	Location	Title	Sponsors	Participants
20 May 1996	Wheaton, IL	Western Assistance for Post-Soviet Seminaries: A Consultation on Strategies	Institute for East-West Christian Studies; Overseas Council	22 Westerners
9-13 Sept. 1996	Kyiv, Ukraine	Consultation on Theological Education	Overseas Council; Peter Deyneka Russian Ministries	94 (64 from FSU, 30 foreigners)
13 Oct. 1997	Moscow, Russia	Consultation on Theological Education	Overseas Council; Peter Deyneka Russian Ministries; Eurasian Accrediting Association	Approximately 120, including 20 Westerners
4-5 May 1998	Kyiv, Ukraine	Seminar on Preparation of Accreditation Commissions	Eurasian Accrediting Association	25, including 2 Westerners
16-18 June 1998	St. Petersburg, Russia	Conference on Alternative Theological Education	St. Petersburg Christian University; Oxen Ministries; Study by Extension for All Nations (SEAN)	Approximately 40, including 12 Westerners
1-5 Sept. 1998	Osijek, Croatia	Equipping Kingdom Leaders for the 21st Century: Consultation of Theological Education on Leadership Development in the Post-Communist World	Council for Eastern European Theological. Education (CEETE); Overseas Council; International Fellowship of Missionary Theologians (INFEMIT)	80-100 from ECE; 20 INFEMIT leaders from around the world; 30 Westerners

| 19-23 October 1998 | Donetsk, Ukraine | Administration, Governing, and Finance of Educational Institutions | Eurasian Accrediting Association | |

Editor's Notes for Appendix:

1. In August 1990 Biblical Education by Extension hosted an interdenominational conference in Vienna, Austria. While not addressing specifically post-Soviet theological education, it did focus on pastoral training, and it did include participants from East Central Europe and the Soviet Union.
2. In October 1993 the Southern Baptist Foreign Mission Board sponsored a theological conference for Evangelical Christians-Baptists which explored the need for a seminary and Bible school accrediting association.
3. In October 1994 the organizing committee of the future Eurasian Accrediting Association, along with St. Petersburg Christian University and Odessa Theological Seminary, sponsored an academic conference on the history of Evangelical Christians-Baptists in Russia in St. Petersburg. The approximately 50 participants included about five westerners.
4. The Smolensk Orthodox Seminary and the Synodal Education Committee of the Moscow Patriarchate sponsored an international conference on "Theological Education: Traditions and Development," 24-25 September 1997 in Smolensk. For a conference summary see "Church News" in the Russian Orthodox Church website: http://www.russian-orthodox-church.org.ru/ne311074.htm.
5. The Eurasian Accrediting Association has sponsored two meetings on theological library development. A third is scheduled for 19-23 October 1998 in Chisinau (Kishinev), Moldova.

SECTION 3

EMERGING CONCERNS

CHAPTER 7
POST-SOVIET PROTESTANT THEOLOGICAL EDUCATION: COME OF AGE? (1999)

From not a single Evangelical seminary in the Soviet Union in 1986 to over 100 on its former territory today, and from no residential students to some 3,000 today, this has to rank as one of the more dramatic developments in leadership training in the history of Protestantism. The opportunity for a fresh appraisal of this phenomenon came with a conference of Protestant theological educators, held near Kyiv, Ukraine, 9-12 September 1996. Ninety-four delegates (64 from the former Soviet Union and 30 from the West) celebrated the graduation of nine seminarians from the firstever Russian M.A. program in Protestant theological studies, a joint effort of Odessa Theological Seminary, St. Petersburg Christian University, and Donetsk Christian University. (See the *East-West Church & Ministry Report* 4: Fall 1996, p. 14 for the names of candidates and titles of theses). Delegates also witnessed substantive theological discussion, growing indigenous leadership, and the launching of a Protestant theological accrediting association with a wide-ranging, ambitious agenda.

Among indigenous conference participants, the average number of years of involvement in theological education was three/ a startling illustration of the infancy of the movement. Nevertheless, W estern observers who had attended the first such gathering in February 1993 in Moscow and the second in October I 994 in Oradea, Romania, commented on the rapid maturation and growing sophistication of the indigenous leadership.[1]

Reprinted with permission from *The Asbury Theological Journal* 54 (Fall 1999): 37-40.

One theme that seminary representatives frequently voiced was the need for close ties to the church. Peter Penner of St. Petersburg Christian University (SPCU1, in his "Current Analysis of Theological Education," stated,

> Seminaries need to work with the church. The question is how closely. At first, St Petersburg Christian University did not emphasize church relations. Then we came to understand that we exist for the church; the church does not exist for the seminary. Now, the president of the Evangelical Christian-Baptist Union of Russia is on the SPCU board Now we emphasize student work in churches and church recommendations for students. SPCU has had conferences for the pastors of its students and has asked pastors how SPCU can help students not to become arrogant.

Aleksei Melnichuk, Donetsk Christian University, made similar points in his review of "Issues in Church/School Relationships," as did Anatoly Prokopchuk of Kyiv Evangelical Christian-Baptist (ECB) Seminary: "Be close to the church. It doesn't matter what the level of education of the school. Independent schools produce graduates 'who are on the street' with no church to go to. ECB churches may not accept these graduates."

As the present massive level of Western assistance subsides over time, the new seminaries will become ever more aware of their need for close ties with local churches, not only for reasons of placement but for financial support. At present however, church contributions to theological education in the former Soviet Union are quite limited. As Aleksei Melnichuk noted, many churches are in building programs that are stretching their capacities to the limit. In addition, a lack of a tradition of stewardship and current chaotic economic conditions spell limited financial support from believers for local churches, much less for more distant seminaries. At present for example, the vast majority of Evangelical churches do not support fulltime ministers. All but six of 75 ECB pastors in the Odessa region have secular employment. Gregori Kommendant president of the Ukrainian ECB, hopes half of the churches under his charge will support their own pastors by the year 2000. Peter Deyneka Russian Ministries sponsored a first-ever Protestant conference on stewardship in Moscow, 24-26 October 1996, but more such efforts will be needed

Peter Penner noted that "Many schools live just one day at a time. Many administrators just settle [immediate] crises." One of these crises that received attention at the Kyiv consultation concerned enrollment. Pressure is mounting to enlarge student bodies, not to increase revenue from quite modest tuition, but at least partly to justify each school's existence in the eyes of Western benefactors. As a result, schools increasingly are competing for students. Two Western doctoral candidates currently researching post-Soviet Protestant theological education have shared with this reporter that academic standards have suffered in the process. Peter Konovalchik, president of the Russian ECB federation, contended, quite justifiably, that the need now is not to start more schools, but to strengthen existing ones.

In a debriefing session for Western participants, Jack Graves, Director of Research for Overseas Council for Theological Education, observed that "schools need quickly to move from dependency to financial independence for there to be true independence." Indigenous speakers in general sessions made the same argument. Anatoly Prokopchuk, for example, urged self-sufficiency: "We thank our brothers from the West for help. But now we need to think of supporting ourselves. And our Western brothers will rejoice, too."

One reason Protestant leaders in the former Soviet Union fear the present overwhelming Western influence upon theological education, quietly if not publicly, is theological. Although the issue did not emerge in plenary sessions, they do consider a minority of Western instructors to be liberal. Especially troubling to them are those guest professors who they feel question the authority of Scripture. Also, Protestant leaders recognize that a majority of Western instructors are Calvinists, which is not to their liking. Anatoly Prokopchuk put it bluntly: "We have a problem with liberalism and Calvinism." Aleksei Melnichuk explained it this way:

> Seminary graduates often criticize [Russian and Ukrainian] Baptist traditions. Western teachers are seen as the source of much of this criticism. Students will ask a Western professor about eternal security and students will accept the Western professor's eternal security teaching over their home pastors' freewill position that is not argued in an educated manner.

It should be noted that the majority of Western Evangelicals active in post-Soviet ministry are Calvinists, although most do not emphasize the fact and many incorrectly presume, consciously or unconsciously, that *Evangelical* and *Reformed* are synonyms. That Wesleyan Arminian and Pentecostal interpretations may equally be deemed Evangelical often does not occur to Calvinists in the West. For their part, a majority of Slavic Evangelicals, Baptists as well as Pentecostals, are Arminian, although they typically do not use this term. Naturally, this difference gives rise to considerable tension, and nowhere more quickly than in Western assistance to post-Soviet seminaries.

Slavic Protestant leaders contend not only with Western theological influences that they consider harmful, but they also contend in their own ranks with strong anti-intellectual currents that view all theological education with suspicion. Pavel Damian, a Christian publisher from St. Petersburg, noted that many pastors still feel that the only book their congregations need to read is the Bible. Sergei Rybikov of the Christian Missionary Union in south Russia reiterated the "negative view of education" in many churches. Peter Penner shared that he had written ninety pages defending the spiritual value of instruction and study. In contrast, the opening address of the conference by a Baptist elder statesman launched a thinly-veiled attack on study in the West modern Bible translations, and "intellectualism" in general. While one might be disappointed with this lack of understanding of the life of the mind in the service of Christendom, it is sensible to be wary of Western theological education for Slavic seminarians *en masse,* and it is sensible to be wary of unwarranted prestige that can lead believers to prefer professors over pastors. Dallas Seminary professor Mark Young noted, "If [seminary] teachers have little contact with churches and pastors, then most students will want to be professors, not pastors." One Western doctoral candidate surveying post-Soviet seminarians has already documented an alarmingly widespread preference among Slavic seminarians for teaching over preaching.

Yet concern over Western influences in seminaries is not only theological; it also is political. Some leaders fear the loss of control as Western notions of democratic procedure and freedom of speech seep into the consciousness of newly-educated pastors. One delegate at the conference, fearing that church members might contract false notions from various new publications, asked the head of Ukrainian Evangelical Christians-Baptists, "Is it possible to control the literature we are printing?" When Rev. Kommendant responded that today it is impossible, applause followed. He continued, "What fruit is sweet? What is prohibited? Some books should be burned, but we cannot do that "freedom is freedom." At the same time, Russian ECB president Konovalchik volunteered a more traditional attitude. We need some control. For example, I saw a Pentecostal book in a Baptist kiosk. We cannot trust all publishing houses."

Konovalchik's negative reference to Pentecostals leads to a shortcoming of a conference billed as interdenominational: 76.5 percent of participants were Evangelical Christians-Baptists but Pentecostals, arguably as large as the ECB in the former Soviet Union, accounted for only five percent. On the one hand, conference sponsors, Overseas Council for Theological Education and Peter Deyneka Russian Ministries, sincerely desired broad representation from all Evangelical denominations and all Pentecostal seminaries and Bible institutes received invitations. On the other hand, the indigenous organizing committee for the conference and the program itself included no Pentecostals. This reporter learned after the conference, Pentecostals perceived the function to be a Baptist undertaking and most apparently declined to participate as a result. While many Western observers at the conference were pained by various critical comments from Baptists about Pentecostals not to mention about Calvinistsit must be noted, sadly, that Pentecostal disdain for non-Pentecostals in the former Soviet Union is at least as intense.

On a more positive note, after considerable discussion, the conference voted to establish a Protestant accrediting association that will be interdenominational rather than exclusively Baptist. In addition, lest the organizing committee be all ECB, Gennadi Sergienko, a young professor from the Moscow ECB Seminary trained at Dallas Seminary, nominated Pentecostal Anatoly Gloukhovsky, who was duly included. Others named to the organizing committee were Aleksei Brynza, R. Kheibulin, Nikolai Kornilov, Aleksei Melnichuk, Fyodor Mokan, Peter Penner, Anatoly Prokopchuk, Vladimir Ryaguzov, Sergei Rybikov, and Sergei Sannikov. The new Protestant theological association will seek affiliation with the International Council for Evangelical Theological Education (ICETE).

Notes

[1] The present report is a continuation of the author's study of the history of and current developments in Russian Protestant theological education: Mark Elliott, "Protestant Education in the Former Soviet Union." *International Bulletin of Missionary Research* 18 (January 1994): 14-22; and Mark Elliott, "Theological Education After Communism: The Mixed Blessing of Western Assistance." *The Asbury Theological Journal* 50 (Spring 1995): 67-73. For a Russian reprint, see: "Bogoslovskoe obrazovanie v postkommunisticheskii period: polozhitel'nye i otritsatel'nye storony zapadooi pomoshchi." *Put' bogopoznaniia*, no. 1 (1996): 17-25.

Chapter 8

Globalization in Theological Education: A Mixed Blessing (2004)

History of the Globalization Initiative

The globalization initiative of the Association of Theological Schools (ATS) began in 1980 with the appointment of a Committee on International Theological Education, later renamed the Committee on Globalization.[1] At the 1986 biennial meeting, ATS extended its commitment to this effort with the appointment of a new Task Force on Globalization. At that gathering, Hispanic theologian Orlando Costas (Andover Newton Theological School) proposed that "the attention of a seminary to its global context" become one of the criteria for ATS accreditation. The passage of this motion led to the implementation of a formal globalization standard in 1990. As revised in 1996, it became "one of four general themes cross-cutting all ATS accrediting standards."[2] With generous grants from the Pew Charitable Trusts, ATS in the 1980s and 90s organized and funded conferences, workshops, surveys, faculty summer sessions, and a variety of individual and faculty team grants on globalization. The Association's journal, *Theological Education*, published prodigiously on the theme: 69 articles between 1986 and 1999 in 9 theme issues devoted exclusively to globalization.[3]

Rationale for the Globalization Initiative

The launching of this global initiative, the most sustained and intensive in the history of ATS, stemmed in large measure from a growing

---

Reprinted with permission from *Christian Education Journal*, Series 3, Vol. 1 (No. 3, 2004): 129-39.

uneasiness with theological education that seemed increasingly insular and parochial. As ATS Executive Director Daniel O. Aleshire put it:

> In the early 1980s...the perception was that North American theological education was focused primarily on North American and Western European theology and church history.
>
> The syllabi of biblical, theology, and history courses in ATS schools tended to be limited to the long history of scholarly work in Europe and North America. But the world was changing; the centers of energy and growth in Christian communities were moving away from North America to South America, Africa, and Asia.... Theological education's primary concentration on the European church, its North American emigrant manifestations, and the religious movements indigenous to North America began to appear non-academic and not faithful to broader religious realities (p. 27).[4]

Paralleling the worldwide growth of the church, especially in Africa, Latin American, and China, was the explosion in the last decades of the 20th century of non-Western missionary outreach, such that at the dawn of the third millennium, not only were the majority of Christians non-Western, but the majority of Christian evangelists and missionaries were non-Western.[5] This new coloration of the Christian community is bound to have an impact on North American theological education—or at least, it can be argued, it should.

In the 1980s and 90s, communication and transportation advances continued to shrink the world and accelerate interdependence. At the same time, for better and worse—because not everyone benefits—an increasingly global economy did the same. Meanwhile, some events that ATS could not have foreseen reinforced the timeliness of its call for greater global consciousness in theological education: the end of Soviet hegemony in Eastern Europe, the astounding dissolution of the Soviet Union itself in 1991, and the end of the Cold War and a bipolar world.[6]

According to a recent study, the United States is "the most religiously diverse nation in the world."[7] Wave upon wave of immigration has made cross-cultural understanding a necessity of human relations, across town and across the back fence, as well as across oceans. North American seminary graduates serving as pastors and their parishioners need a global and cross-cultural comprehension in order to be witnesses who are both compelling and simultaneously tolerant and courteous to those outside the fold of Christian faith. Balancing bold proclamation and respect for freedom of conscience takes finely tuned cross-culture sensitivity. It also takes love for all God's children. And this sensitivity and love are best nurtured in a community of theological education that genuinely values a multicultural and global consciousness.

On an ominous note, European theologian Hans Küng has warned, "There will be no peace on earth without peace among the religions of the world."[8] In a more positive vein, one globalization survey respondent put it this way:

> After all is said and done, it's a matter of faith! This is an ongoing struggle, but the struggle to achieve the Kingdom of God is a part of life. The commitment to cross-cultural understanding is part of the commitment of living in a Christian community. Once you accept the fact, then you have no choice but to do the very best you can.[9]

Terminology and Definitions

Following criticism of the term *international* for connoting a nation-state and political frame of reference, ATS settled on *globalization* as the preferred designation for its campaign to combat parochialism in theological education. As it turned out, deciding on the term proved to be far easier than defining it. Don Browning, at the 1986 ATS meeting, delineated what has become an oft-repeated, fourfold typology of options: Globalization can mean: (a) worldwide evangelism, and/or (b) ecumenism, and/or (c) inter-faith dialogue, and/or (d) improving the lives of the world's poor and disadvantaged.[10]

As globalization evolved from an initiative into an accreditation standard, it became absolutely critical that ATS, as a matter of institutional survival, allow its dramatically diverse constituency to determine on an individual basis the parameters for the term. As long-term globalization task force director William E. Lesher noted, "Quite consciously" the task force "fended off calls to produce a sharper definition of globalization…in the hope that the variety of participants would continue to be engaged."[11] It could be argued that pragmatism prevailed over logic, because the options "are not different shades of meaning of a broad construct," as Executive Director Aleshire put it, "they represent fundamentally different, even opposing meanings."[12] If, for example, interfaith dialogue for Aleshire requires that Christianity "no longer have its old privilege and presumption of finality,"[13] how can that possibly be squared with "the church's universal mission to evangelize the world, i.e., to take the message of the gospel to all people, all nations, all cultures, and all religious faiths."[14]

Globalization as an accrediting standard within a body as pluralistic as ATS has the potential to be disruptive and divisive because, if defined in only one or two of the four ways, it could become "*doctrinally* unacceptable to many schools."[15] The meaning of globalization in an ATS that is both Protestant and Catholic, and both mainline and evangelical, may not devolve to the lowest common denominator—none may exist. Rather, each institution agrees upon definitions for globalization for its own purposes. And as a consequence, the conclusion seems unavoidable that globalization, which can be defined so many different ways, lacks precision and clear focus. Noting this definitional disarray is not to suggest that globalization is unimportant—far from it. It does suggest that a school must take great care in crafting its own definition, because with no clear common ground, the possibility looms large for one or more of an institution's constituencies to misconstrue the purpose of a globalization emphasis.

Further Reservations

In the same year that ATS formally concluded its globalization initiative, the spring 1999 issue of the journal, *Theological Education*, offered many valuable insights on the subject. At the same time, it unfortunately was nearly bereft of evangelical reflection. Robert Ferrit (Columbia International University) was the only clearly identifiable evangelical contributor in this 189-page volume. Mainline and Catholic predominance helps explain the presence of recommendations that prove objectionable to evangelicals, such as the need, according to M. Thomas Thangaraj of Candler School of Theology, for "the reinterpretation of certain 'exclusive' texts within the Bible."[16] Max Stackhouse (1988), who contributed to this volume, elsewhere dramatically dismissed a cherished evangelical presupposition when he wrote, "So long, *sola scriptura.*"[17]

When some ATS members see the exclusive claims of Scripture as negotiable and others see them as non-negotiable, globalization is bound to mean apples and oranges. And with such a vast degree of imprecision inherent in the definition and in the exercise, the value of combating parochialism in theological education still exists, but any consensus as to the necessary antidote seems remote indeed. Notwithstanding the ambiguity of definition and scant evangelical representation in the spring 1999 issue of *Theological Education* on globalization, evangelicals still have reason to champion the concept to the extent that it underscores Christ's call to minister to body and soul in all the earth.

Despite a massive, prodigious, decades-long effort by ATS to fortify and incorporate a global consciousness into its life, globalization still has its detractors. Oddly enough, the church growth movement's deference to the principle of homogeneity (like attracts like), and the advent of the megachurch with its focus on front door ease of entry, can obscure the necessity of cross-cultural ministry.[18] Immediate practicality also informs the mindset of a portion of theological students who question the vocational relevance of cross-cultural experiences and any global component in a seminary curriculum.[19] Candidates for the ministry need to be instructed in love that the best medicine for any local church is the tonic of witness and godly compassion directed beyond its four walls. When a hungry and hurting world lost in sin is the focus of a congregation, internal feuds over mode of worship or the color of new carpet pale in significance and lose their power to divide and conquer.

The reservations of seminary faculty, though muted before the juggernaut of Pew-funded globalization, also deserve consideration. Academics trained in Western universities with Western curricula based on Western scholarship are not easily tempted to rethink their education, their teaching, and their research interests. Church history surveys, for example, typically trace developments "from Jerusalem to Athens to Rome to Wittenburg to Geneva," with minimal attention paid to the history of Christianity in Africa, Asia, and Latin America.[20] Or take the example of biblical studies. All churches, old and new, East and West, South and North, rightly attach the greatest importance to this discipline, which provides the common foundation for all Christians. But Lesher and Shiver (1999) point out that

> The academic study of the Bible is embodied internationally in various societies most of whose roots and leaders are Europeans and Americans. The thought that Asian and African cultural contexts have original, *substantive* contributions to the interpretation of the Bible did not fall uniformly on receptive ears, including, for example, those of the Society of Biblical Literature (SBL).[21]

In 1990 the SBL convention introduced a new program section on "The Bible in Africa, Asia, and Latin America."[22] but it is of marginal, not mainstream, interest to most North American biblical scholars. Lesher and Shriver would appear to be correct in arguing that the discipline of biblical studies does not especially value "Asian and African perspectives on the Bible as the local corollary of the idea that the Bible belongs to the whole world church and to every local context."[23]

Seminary administrators, even those committed to globalization, must also ask hard, legitimate questions: "How do we justify the human and financial costs of cross-cultural relations? Aren't the faculty already overstretched? How do we fit this additional concern into faculty loads?."[24] Even if a nucleus of faculty commits to the integration of cross-cultural and global perspectives in theological education, countervailing tradition and inertia can short-circuit the enterprise unless administrators commit as well. This involves leading the faculty to a consensus as to (a) what globalization means, (b) what concrete goals will be pursued, and (c) what human and financial resources will be required to realize these goals.[25]

North American churches, seminaries, and faculty all have their reservations, but by far the most adamant opposition to globalization in North American theological education comes, paradoxically, from non-Western Christians. To begin with, the peoples of developing nations do not see the advent of a global economy as an unmitigated asset. New jobs may be created, but where labor laws are weak or nonexistent, workers may be exploited and children may toil long hours for a pittance.[26] And if, as Francis Bacon argued, knowledge is power, then Western dominance of worldwide computer networking accrues primarily to Western advantage. In the same vein, the poor nations of the world may regard Western hegemony in global markets, movies, and music as a "new form of socio-cultural imperialism."[27] Kathryn Poethig (1999) makes the same point in referencing globalization as "unevenness in economic affairs" and "a new form of Western domination."[28] The language can get rough, with indictments of globalization as "an exploitative bazaar of greed" in which a "McWorld" of "American consumerism" reigns.[29] The impetus for free trade that fuels the global economy usually benefits developed Northern economies more than developing Southern economies whose fledgling industries are hard pressed to compete when shorn of protective tariffs.

The global economy is directly germane to theological education because just when the world's poor were becoming wary of the concept of globalization, North American seminaries seemed to be championing this suspect ideology.[30] As Aleshire notes, "What began among the ATS schools as a name for a legitimate effort to de-parochialize theological thinking has ended, in the secular use of the term, as a name for economic developments that have taken a large toll on human well-being."[31]

Just as the non-Western world came to distrust the consequences of globalization, non-Western theological educators have come to distrust globalization in theological education. In a meeting of some 30 African theological educators in Tanzania, one speaker "shouted angrily that globalization was another, perhaps even more devastating, act of North American imperialism." Another speaker dejectedly predicted this Western agenda would detract from or even usurp growing and fruitful Third World explorations of theological contextualization.[32] Paradoxically, in the name of better world understanding, the West was feared to be undermining non-Western efforts to better understand the gospel in non-Western contexts.[33] Because of the negative connotations of globalization in the non-Western world, the ATS task force "shifted its use of terms, no longer using the noun 'globalization' to characterize ATS school activities and initiatives, and instead using terms such as 'responses to globalization' or 'global activities' of theological education."[34]

It can be argued that Pew-funded globalization for North American seminaries actually undermined Christian leadership development in the rest of the world to the extent that indigenous faculty and seminarians were drawn to the West to "diversify" majority white campuses. The reason is that the rate of repatriation has been shockingly low. One study found that 90%

of Asian Indian theological students who studied in the West never went home. The figures for Colombia and the Caribbean were nearly as troubling: 75-85%.[35] A missionary to North Africa shared with this writer that of 42 Moroccan seminarians who had studied abroad, only two had returned home.[36] One contributor to the globalization theme issue, Judith Berling, to her credit devoted a paragraph to this problem.[37] Otherwise, the seductive and destructive lure of the West, which amounts to a Third World theological brain drain that Pew-funded globalization tended to exacerbate, received no mention in the spring 1999 isue of *Theological Education*. Even when graduates do return home, the Western education they received frequently translates poorly into non-Western contexts.[38]

Next Steps

North American seminaries concerned with globalization in theological education, which do not want to undermine church leadership development outside the West, should consider the advice of Judith A. Berling (Graduate Theological Union, Berkeley, CA), director of the ATS Incarnating Globalization Project, in her two excellent articles from the globalization theme issue entitled "Collective Wisdom" and "Getting Down to Cases."[39] She offers a wealth of quite practical advice for incorporating global perspectives and cross-cultural experience in theological education, based on the experience of various seminaries that have undertaken globalization initiatives.

Developing Institutional Commitment

1. Schools should be realistic about the substantial costs of cross-cultural relationships in terms of budget, faculty, and administration. Effective global or local cross-cultural partnerships "cannot be a one-year experiment." To work, they require long-term commitment, time, and energy.[40]

2. To succeed, all seminary stakeholders need to see cross-cultural partnerships as part of the school's mission.[41]

3. "Institutional ownership comes from actual cross-cultural experience."[42] And to sustain it, faculty, as well as students, should be involved.

4. To be sustained over time, cross-cultural programs must be more than periodic "enrichment opportunities." They must be embedded in the curriculum.[43]

Developing Global Connections

5. Schools should carefully consider their existing cross-cultural and global ties. The best building blocks may be the heightened awareness and concern of faculty and alumni who have already been involved in cross-cultural experiences.[44]

Developing Trust and Mutuality with Partners

6. A school must invest significant time in order to develop a cross-cultural partnership worthy of the name. To "build mutual relationships" a North American seminary must enter into "ongoing conversations" that involve "time…spent at the site(s) where programmatic aspect(s) of the relationship will be implemented." The Western assumption is that relationships are "quickly realizable," whereas potential non-Western partners will "have a different sense of time and [will] see relationships as developing slowly over a long history of give and take."[45]

7. "Seminaries need to be particularly wary of using other communities for their own purposes. Both parties should benefit from a cross-cultural relationship and each should understand the needs and the stakes of the other. Before committing to a short-term experience, school decision-makers should consider seriously any long-term expectations from its partner communities or cultures."[46]

8. Finally, schools need to be aware of the dangers of "asymmetry" in financial arrangements in cross-cultural partnerships. Where such relationships have worn thin or been severed, the culprit often is the Western side's unknowing insensitivity to the one-sidedness of the arrangement. "A sense of indebtedness or of being the client of a wealthy patron has inhibited international or cross-cultural partners from expressing their needs, concerns, and stakes. North American schools need to be aware of this

historical dynamic." Non-Western partners, typically struggling financially, "are often too polite to assert their own agenda or challenge the unconscious assertion of privilege, which can so easily come with the resources and good intentions of North American institutions."[47]

Overcoming Enduring Provincialism

A good case can be made that the ATS globalization initiative was self-serving. It was fundamentally about strengthening North American, not non-Western, theological education. As a result, unless care is taken, it can be a bitter irony to see the awakening of Western institutions to global realities accomplished at the expense of the rest of the globe. Terry Provance of the United Church Board for World Ministries was right to warn that "the North cannot approach the South as a mine from which it can resource its religious crisis of meaning and identity."[48] Likewise, Fumitaka Matsuoka of the Pacific School of Religion cautioned, "Even as we search for a new paradigm of cross-culturally sensitive global understanding, we sometimes slip back into old habits of privilege; for example, when the transformation of North Americans is structured to take place at the expense of the people elsewhere who serve as agents of 'transformation.'"[49]

Could it be symptomatic of the West's enduring provincialism in Christian leadership training that the ATS flagship journal, *Theological Education*, still considers for publication only articles "devoted to the distinctive concerns of graduate theological education in North America."[50] To be sure, many scores of articles on globalization have been granted exemptions. Nevertheless, that two decades of ATS focus on globalization have not rescinded this editorial policy does not speak well for the depth of the Association's transformation in global awareness to date. Again, paradoxically, one of the best exercises North American seminaries could possibly undertake on their own behalf would be to study exceptional non-Western theological programs that evidence creativity and dynamism. Residential seminaries in Russia, for example, typically lack endowments, proper facilities, adequately trained faculty, and libraries worthy of the name, but students and instructors there often have a thirst for acquiring and imparting God's truths and a zeal for ministry that would be the envy of any North American seminary. Unfortunately, such accounts will be rarities[51] unless *Theological Education* changes its submission policy.

Notes

1. Lesher, W. and Shriver, D. (1999). "Stumbling in the Right Direction." *Theological Education*, 35 (2), 3.

2. Lesher and Shriver, "Stumbling," 4-5.

3. Lesher and Shriver, "Stumbling," 4-5. Also Schreiter, R. J. (1999). "Forward." Theological Edu-cation, 35 (2), v-vi and "A Decade of Special Issues in Theological Education" (1999). *Theological Education*, 35 (2), 79-84.

4. Aleshire, D. O. (1999). "Words and Deeds: An Informal Assessment of Globalization in Theo-logical Education." *Theological Education*, 35 (2), 27.

5. Walls, A. F. (1996). "Missiological Education in Historical Perspective" in J. D. Woodbury (ed.), *Missiological Education in the Twenty-First Century: The Book, the Circle, and the Sandals*. Maryknoll, NY: Orbis, 18.

6. Schreiter, "Forward,"v-vi, and Thangaraj, T. M. (1999). "Globalization, World Religions, and Theological Education." *Theological Education*, 35 (2), 144.

7. Lesher and Shriver, "Stumbling," 11.

8. Cited in Lesher and Shriver, "Stumbling," 12.

9. Berling, J. A. (1999). "Collective Wisdom: What ATS Schools Have Learned about Establishing, Sustaining, and Evaluating Good Cross-cultural Relationships." *Theological Education*, 35 (2), 98.

10. Lesher and Shriver, "Stumbling," 6.

11. Ibid., 7.

12. Aleshire, "Words and Deeds," 29.

13. Ibid.

14. Browning, D. S. (1986). "Globalization and the Task of Theological Education in North Ameri-ca." *Theological Education*, 23 (1), 43.

15. Aleshire, "Words and Deeds," 29.

16. Thangaraj, "Globalization," 151.

17. Stackhouse, M. L. (1988). *Apologia: Contextualization, Globalization, and Mission in Theolog-ical Education*. Grand Rapids, MI: Eerdmans, 50.

18. Lesher and Shriver, "Stumbling," 13.

19. Berling, "Collective Wisdom," 91-92.

20. Lesher and Shriver, "Stumbling," 5-6.

21. Ibid., 6.

22. Ibid., 15.

23. Ibid., 6.

24. Berling, "Collective Wisdom," 96.

25. Ibid., 87-88.

26. Aleshire, "Words and Deeds," 29-30.

27. Stackhouse, M. L., (1999). "Globalization, Faith, and Theological Education." *Theological Education*, 35 (2), 69.

28. Poethig, K. (1999). "The Calculus of Global Culture." *Theological Education*, 35 (2), 40.

29. Stackhouse, "Globalization," 69.

30. Matsuoka, F. (1999). "The Changing Terrain of Globalization in ATS Conversations." *Theological Education*, 35 (2), 20.

31. Aleshire, "Words and Deeds," 30.

32. Lesher, W., and Zikmund, B. B. (1999). "Resistance to the Globalization Emphasis in ATS Schools from Theological Educators from Other Parts of the World." *Theological Education*, 35 (2), 181.

33. Ibid., 181-182.

34. Matsuoka, "Changing Terrain," 19.

35. Graves, J. (1992). "Plugging the Theological Brain Drain." *Evangelical Missions Quarterly*, 28, 154-161.

36. Anonymous missionary, personal communication, January 7, 2000.

37. Berling, J. A. (1999). "Getting Down to Cases: Responses to Globalization in ATS Schools." *Theological Education*, 35 (2), 110.

38. Berling, "Collective Wisdom," 97. Also Lesher and Zikmund, "Resistance," 182.

39. Berling, "Collective Wisdom" and Berling, "Getting Down to Cases."

40. Berling, "Getting Down to Cases," 136.

41. Berling, "Collective Wisdom," 87.

42. Ibid., 87.

43. Ibid., 92.

44. Ibid., 87-88.

45. Ibid., 89.

46. Ibid., 90.

47. Berling, "Getting Down to Cases," 111.

48. Cited in Berling, "Getting Down to Cases," 110.

49. Matsuoka, "Changing Terrain," 22.

50. *Theological Education*, 2004, ii.

51. Berling, "Getting Down to Cases," 121-122.

SECTION 4

FUTURE PROMISE AND WARNINGS

CHAPTER 9
THE CURRENT CRISIS IN PROTESTANT THEOLOGICAL EDUCATION IN THE FORMER SOVIET UNION (2010)

Declining Enrollment...

From 1993 to 2007 New Life Bible College in Moscow graduated more than 200 students in a program focused on evangelism, missions, and pastoral ministry.[1] However, this Campus Crusade-sponsored seminary closed its doors following its May 2007 commencement.[2]

In 2009 two other Moscow seminaries of Korean origin, one headed by Gennady Sergienko and another headed by Vladimir Lee, closed their doors.[3] Across the former Soviet Union many residential seminary buildings, built at great expense, are now nearly bereft of full-time students. Missiologist and Russian church historian Walter Sawatsky notes, "Beautiful campuses built largely with largesse from the West, including many thousands of sweat hours by volunteers from America, are standing nearly empty" because of "the near total disappearance of the full-time student."[4] From the Baltic to the Pacific one finds Protestant schools struggling with an enrollment shortfall that threatens their survival. Making matters worse, beleaguered Protestant seminaries from Moscow to Siberia report increasing pressures from local authorities, the mafia, and the Russian Orthodox church.[5] Because conditions are so difficult for Bible colleges in Central Asia, several are contemplating closure or a move to a less hostile environment.[6]

Reprinted with permission from *Religion in Eastern Europe* 30 (November 2010): 1-22.

... Following Dramatic Growth

The current phenomenon of Protestant seminaries under siege stands in stark contrast to the earlier dramatic flowering of formal pastoral training programs as the Soviet regime tottered and then collapsed. Programs grew from not a single Protestant residential seminary in 1986 to 42 programs by 1992, to well over 100 by the end of the 1990s.[7] A 1999 directory of theological institutions listed 137 Protestant, 57 Orthodox, and 4 Catholic schools, while in 2001 Overseas Council International indentified 230 Protestant, 117 Orthodox, and 31 Catholic theological training programs.[8] Growth appears to have continued into the new century. Even today, the Assemblies of God report 135 Pentecostal Bible schools in Russia and Ukraine[9] and the Evangelical Christian-Baptist (ECB) press service estimates 150 ECB-related seminaries and Bible schools across the former Soviet Union.[10]

Overbuilding

In accounting for the current troubles in theological education, however, the large number of Protestant institutions looms large. "Oversaturation of evangelical schools," as David Hoehner, former academic dean at Donetsk Christian University, calls it,[11] stems from many decades of pentup demand, a "time is short" mentality, willing Western donors, and the preference of myriads of Western churches and ministries for "their own independent training programs."[12] Duplication and overbuilding would appear to be the consequence. For example, can Donetsk, Ukraine, with a predominantly secular or Orthodox population, sustain five evangelical pastoral training programs?[13]

The Waning of Church Growth

Initially, new Protestant seminaries benefitted from growing numbers of converts and new churches opening their doors. But denominational reports and mission newsletters have been better at counting those coming in through front doors than in counting those leaving through back doors. Perhaps a half million Evangelicals have emigrated to the West from the former Soviet Union; in addition, some worshippers only darkened church doors temporarily out of short-lived curiosity.[14] With overall church growth waning, enrollments naturally suffer.[15] On the other hand, where church growth continues, as with Pentecostals in Ukraine, Siberia, and the Russian Far East, seminary enrollments have not declined as much, or they continue to rise.[16] Another exception to the rule is Zaporozhe Bible School, which has maintained its enrollment and currently is engaged in a building campaign.[17] Also weathering the crisis well is Moscow Evangelical Christian Seminary, sponsored by U.S.-based OMS International. It enjoyed its largest enrollment of 103 students in fall 2009. This Wesleyan school owns its own property; it has benefitted from strong indigenous and Western leadership and faculty; and it accepts Pentecostal students—41 percent in 2008. Still, fall 2010 enrollment included only 36 residential students, more than other Protestant programs in Moscow, but hardly sustainable as a residential program without enrollment improvements in the future.[18]

Shortcomings in Seminary Candidates

Charley Warner, advisor to the Euro-Asian Accrediting Association (E-AAA), traces the origin of the current enrollment crisis as far back as 1993. At fault, at least in part, he argues, has been competition for students undermining the ability of programs to graduate mature, capable pastors.[19] Peter Mitskevich, now president of the Moscow ECB Theological Seminary, and former

Western missionary Mark Harris have noted various shortcomings in seminary candidates that they have observed firsthand. Some students:

1. are too young to fully absorb instruction;
2. are too inexperienced to apply their learning;
3. lack a clear call to ministry and lack direction in their lives;
4. require elementary discipleship;
5. lack vital connections with home churches;
6. are less concerned with an education than with a diploma;
7. are fascinated with the West, seek to practice English, obtain scholarships to study abroad,
8. and/or emigrate to the West; and
9. have no interest in pastoring, aspiring instead to careers in teaching.[20]

Metropolitan Hilarion, now head of the Moscow Patriarchate Department of External Relations, noted questionable qualifications among some Orthodox seminarians as well. One student, when quizzed on the number of Persons in the Holy Trinity, answered, "One Person." "My next question was, 'Why, then, do we believe in the Trinity if there is only One person in it?' He said, 'Father, I asked you not to ask me any difficult questions, for I am a novice and I have no time to study.' And this is not a made-up funny story; it is a case out of my own teaching practice."[21]

Unfortunately, the strongest potential candidates frequently are pastors too deeply enmeshed in family and ministry responsibilities and too far afield to enroll in full-time, residential programs.[22] With all the pitfalls in student selection, it nevertheless should be emphasized that many godly students have enrolled, have taken their studies to heart, have learned, have been faithfully mentored by their teachers, and have gone on to labor successfully in the Lord's vineyard.

The Church-School Divide

However, with so many students uncertain of their call to ministry and lacking strong ties with a local church, it is no wonder that a seminary-church disconnect exists. Theological educator Taras Dyatlik's survey of 70 pastors found that almost all complained of poor church-seminary relations.[23] Evgeni Bakhmutsky, newly elected ECB deputy chairman, stated back in 2005 that "most of these schools are not really church-oriented" and that pastors "see many difficulties and divisions that are caused by graduates" who have no heart for "sacrificed ministry."[24] For Walter Sawatsky it is a case of "free floating" schools lacking substantive relationships with the churches they seek to serve.[25] Sergei Golovin, director of the Christian Center for Science and Apologetics, flatly states, a "theological school with no connection with local churches is meaningless. Local churches also do not realize that they have no future without theological education" because they easily can fall prey to distortions of the gospel. "As a result, neither our schools view themselves as a part of church, nor local churches see the need for the schools."[26] At a Euro-Asian Accrediting Association (E-AAA) meeting in 1998, one participant warned, "We don't want to have seminaries and churches going in different directions and criticizing each other (as in the West)."[27]

A Lack of Practical Emphasis

The church-school divide has been especially pronounced in those seminaries that have emphasized, or have been perceived to emphasize, academics over practical, pastoral training. Thus, Jason Ferenczi, vice-president of Overseas Council International (OCI), links the enrollment crisis, in part, to inappropriate curricula lacking relevance to ministerial practice.[28] Likewise, Anatoly Prokopchuk (Kyiv Evangelical Christian-Baptist Seminary) speaks of the danger of "the exclusively academic approach" to theological education.[29]

Too often in Orthodox seminaries as well, a tragic "divorce between Christian theory and praxis" prevails, according to Metropolitan Hilarion.[30] A 2007 study of four Ukrainian seminaries edited by E-AAA Executive Director Sergei Sannikov and funded by OCI underscores the point. Twenty percent of surveyed graduates felt their ministerial preparation had been inadequate. Nineteen percent cited "the great difference between what they received [in school] and what is necessary in the local church in ministry." Fourteen percent felt unprepared "to deal with such contemporary issues as abortion, divorce, multiple marriages, homosexuality [and] women's ministry."[31]

Similar shortcomings came to light in Insur Shamgunov's 2008 dissertation based on interviews and surveys of graduates and administrators of four Protestant schools in Kazakhstan and Kyrgyzstan. Respondents "gave generally positive appraisals of their training, but they noted little connection between their studies and the capabilities needed to succeed in ministry."[32] Central Asian church leaders as well noted "a disconnect between current theological training and real-life vocational skills...need[ed] in church ministry."[33] Anyone involved in theological training in the post-Soviet context would do well to note several key findings from Shamgunov's thought provoking research.

1. "In many cases training failed to equip students to integrate classroom studies with practical ministry, it lacked spiritual mentoring, and it placed a disproportionate emphasis upon subjects that had few obvious links to practice."[34]

2. "One of my most surprising findings was that only a quarter of graduates interviewed pointed to cross-cultural issues as bearing any significance for effective learning. Rather, the majority were more concerned with the practical application of what their teachers taught, which in turn was linked not to their teachers' cultural background, but primarily to their practical experience, personal spiritual maturity, and teaching expertise."[35]

3. "The majority of criticisms from graduates were directed not at culturally uncontextualized theological training, but at the larger issue of the theory-practice divide, which is relevant not only to Central Asia, but to theological education everywhere....The challenge seems to be not so much contextualizing theological education for Central Asia, but contextualizing theological education to real-life ministerial practice, regardless of the locale."[36]

Church Distrust of Graduates

Lax admission standards and tenuous church-school ties thus have produced many graduates whom churches and church leaders often deem too young, too inexperienced, too headstrong, and too uncertain of their ministerial call to be trusted in the pulpit. Exacerbating the generation gap and the problem of placement has been an often deep-seated wariness of theological education among pastors and denominational leaders who typically had no chance for formal training in the Soviet era.[37] In addition, some tradition-minded church folk and their shepherds have struggled with resentment and jealousy toward those receiving educational opportunities they never could have imagined. Especially where seminarians have exhibited an "air of superiority" and have studied in residential programs in large cities, they have refused to pastor out-of-the-way, rural congregations.[38]

Alienating seminary graduates from those they are trained to serve has been the suspicion of churches and church leaders that the new seminaries harbor the pox of theological liberalism and Calvinism.[39] The fear has been that graduates might infect mostly conservative Arminian congregations with one or the other contagion of Western origin. Taras Dyatlik's survey of pastors revealed that many equate Calvinism and liberalism and "refuse to send students even to those schools which have only one or two professors who openly espouse Reformed doctrines."[40]

The Disadvantages of Western Funding

Protestant church leaders also frequently distrust seminaries because the schools have been financed overwhelmingly from Western sources. Paradoxically, Western funding has increased the church-school gap, resulting in fewer church placements for graduates, which has meant fewer students enrolling in programs that may not lead to employment. Except for some small, church-based Bible schools, the vast majority of residential training facilities have been underwritten by Western and Korean denominations and missions. Likewise, operating budgets have been heavily dependent upon outside funding. In 2001 Jason Ferenczi of Overseas Council wrote that in the case of 10 schools for which budget data were available, average local funding amounted to 14 percent, "well below averages for other parts of the world."[41] Similarly, Ray Prigodich, former academic dean at Donetsk Christian University, estimated in early 2008 that local funding accounted for some 12 percent of the operating budget at the Moscow Evangelical Christian-Baptist Theological Seminary, 30 percent at Donetsk Christian University, and over 50 percent at Zaoksky Adventist University.[42] Nevertheless, despite some progress, to this day the great majority of Protestant seminaries in the former Soviet Union would quickly close if shorn of Western or Korean support.[43]

Sadly, with outside dependency comes outside control, even if the language of partnership is employed by funders. Theological educators Cheryl and Wesley Brown cite the case of an American mission that finances a post-Soviet seminary on the explicit condition that the funders appoint all indigenous and Western faculty.[44] In another case, a Western mission withdrew its funds and faculty from a fledgling East European seminary because the school could not in good faith subscribe to its benefactor's doctrinal position on eschatology. The Browns characterize such heavy-handed control as "Western theological imperialism."[45] But even outside funders who strive not to be overbearing still exercise a quiet, sometimes even unconscious, check on the prerogatives of indigenous seminary leaders. Unfortunately, what might be termed missiological, rather than Marxist, economic determinism is at work. One East European church leader, observing the power of Western aid in the wake of failed Soviet rule, called to mind a perversion of the Golden Rule: "He who holds the gold, makes the rules."[46]

In sum, church distrust of seminaries jeopardizes their existence because it undermines their ability to recruit students. This distrust, in turn, is partially a function of seminaries answering ultimately to Western donors, rather than to the churches they exist to serve. Respected educational specialist Ted Ward writes,

> When the program is treated as if it were property of the outsiders, local "ownership" and true contextualization become highly unlikely. Westerners in general and Americans in particular seem to prefer high-control management....But we must find ways to encourage those with whom we serve to share in the responsibilities and initiatives of decision-making. To do less is not Christian; it is colonial.[47]

Dieumeme Noelliste, for many years president of the Caribbean Graduate School of Theology, could be speaking as easily for the post-Soviet context as for the global South when he writes, "Northern [or Western] input, though welcome, should be supportive, not determinative." The goal should be "the eventual self sufficiency of southern institutions."[48] To that end, "Real support by the local church which theological education serves is an essential nutrient for its eventual growth from the status of a sheltered garden of foreign dependency to that of a fully acclimatized tree with deep roots in the southern soil."[49]

Seminary Degrees and Unemployment

Protestant residential training programs, then, face an uncertain future because of their overabundance, declining church growth, and weak church-school ties exacerbated by lax admission policies, curricula that appear to be insufficiently practical, and church distrust and lack of ownership of seminaries.[50] Finally, schools are at risk because fewer and fewer prospective students and their parents see reason to invest years of study in programs that rarely lead to self-sustaining employment. More and more, those considering seminary are asking, "Why should I invest three to five years in full-time study so that I can remain poor?"[51] Oleg Turlac and Taras Dyatlik stress the need for graduate placement services, whereas until recently seminary programs gave such a concern little attention.[52]

As it is, the likelihood of low-paying positions, when they can be had, give pause to prospective students. Compounding the problem, years of study and increasing acquaintance with the common Western practice of full-time pastoral positions, have led seminary students to set their sights on full-time church appointments, which actually are quite rare.[53] The malaise affects faculty as well as students. As one out-of-work theology teacher observed: "My children have a bad habit. They like to eat."[54]

Reevaluating a School's Purpose

In coming to terms with the dire straits of most residential programs, E-AAA Executive Director Sergei Sannikov has noted, "There was no strategic plan when these schools were founded—they were spontaneous creations. People were enthusiastic, Western support was available, and so they began."[55] Lack of careful deliberation and forethought does appear to best characterize the launching of many schools. Thus, Moldovan professor Oleg Turlac's advice for a first step forward is for seminaries to "reevaluate their mission and vision. Each school should meet with its association or union of churches to discuss the purpose for the existence of the school and the issue of ministry placement."[56]

Academic Versus Pastoral Training

In a sentence, should theological training be academic, pastoral, or both? Many church leaders in the former Soviet Union would second the conclusion of evangelical Anglican theologian Alister McGrath that "The growing gap between academic theology and the church has led to much theology focusing on issues which appear to be an utter irrelevance to the life, worship, and mission of the church."[57]

Estonian Baptist theologian Toivo Pilli quotes McGrath approvingly, but he also sees a vital role for "academic" theology in "the prophetic task" of producing "contextually relevant theological reflection" on pressing social and cultural issues. Thus, he argues, seminaries "should not be seen only as giving training for church workers;" they are obligated as well to offer "'tools' for the church to fulfill its mission in society."[58]

Budapest-based missiologist Anne Marie Kool recommends theological training that will "give direction" to Christians in how to "relate to the wider society in crucial issues like freedom and morality."⁵⁹ Likewise, Orthodox scholar and theological educator Alexander Bodrov insists that theological education must "answer the questions that the secular society, culture, and science pose.... We cannot and must not become isolated in our tradition, cut off from the rest of the world."⁶⁰

No doubt, some post-Soviet theological educators have become mesmerized with academic learning at the expense of pastoral training—as can happen in the West as well. Still, Toivo Pilli seems justified in rejecting the "growing tendency to see 'faith' and 'knowledge' as contradictory terms."⁶¹ Whatever one concludes on the perennial question of the relationship of faith and knowledge, the point is: Each school and all its stakeholders must think through the question in order to champion a common vision and purpose for each institution.

Responses to Declining Enrollment

As the enrollment crisis has deepened, theological schools have responded in a variety of ways. The most common adjustment to the disappearance of full-time residential students has been to expand non-formal programs—which presently is saving many institutions from closure. The subject of non-formal theological education in the post-Soviet context is so vast that it deserves its own paper or monograph. After enumerating other responses, I will return to this topic.

Closures and Mergers

Lacking students, some programs, as noted, have closed, and more will follow. Even Sergei Sannikov concedes, "The number of theological schools will and must decrease."⁶² It would make sense for some schools to merge. Full-blown theological education is arguably the most expensive enterprise the church undertakes. The development of facilities, faculty, libraries, and textbooks is enormously costly and time-consuming. Given the modest number of Protestants in the former Soviet Union (perhaps one percent of the population), minimal indigenous funding, and the trailing off of Western interest, school mergers would seem a logical necessity. ⁶³

Beyond economic concerns, Dieumeme Noelliste rightly points out, "The merging of weak institutions boosts Christian witness. Clearly, it is much easier for society to ignore a multitude of struggling theological schools."[64] However, tenacious allegiance to denominational and doctrinal distinctives works against such unions. It may be the sad case that some doctrinaire Western sponsors, determining the fate of "their" schools, will prefer closure to what they define as compromise. Still, even short of merger, much fruitful cooperation has occurred through E-AAA, with projects such as a proposed interlibrary loan system promising genuine cost savings.

For those in the former Soviet Union who dare to dream of the miracle of cooperation, the example of the Bulgarian Evangelical Theological Institute (BETI) deserves note. In 1999 in Sofia six denominational schools (Assemblies of God, Baptist, Church of God, Congregational, Methodist, and United Church of God) made common cause to develop a stronger program than any single denomination could manage. While less successful than one would desire, it nevertheless is a model worth consideration.[65]

Finding a Niche

Another seminary survival stratagem will be to develop unique educational specializations.[66] A number of schools in Central and Eastern Europe prepare students to teach religion in public schools.[67] Unlike schools in the former Soviet Union, some seminaries in Poland, the Czech Republic, and Romania receive governmental and European Union support.[68] The Baptist theological faculty in Romania has secured an unusual niche in an Orthodox context as a department in Romania's flagship University of Bucharest.[69]

Turning to the former U.S.S.R., the College of Theology and Education in Chisinau, Moldova, with a focus on outreach to Muslims, has more Central Asian than Moldovan students.[70] The Eurasian Missionary College in Kazan also has a Muslim studies emphasis. The school's former director, Insur Shamgunov, suggests seminaries offer a vocational tract, including such subjects as heating systems and welding.[71] Besides helping fill rosters and balance budgets, such programs could provide seminarians with essential survival skills in bi-vocational ministry.[72]

Some schools have expanded their English language programs to attract additional students. More ambitious has been widespread consideration for the introduction of liberal arts programs parallel to theological studies. Two Central Asian schools in Shamgunov's study were considering this option.[73] In addition to theological education, the Greek Catholic University of Lviv (Ukraine) offers a wide variety of liberal arts programs.[74] Names of seminaries such as St. Petersburg Christian University (SPCU) and Donetsk Christian University (DCU) certainly indicate their intentions to offer non-theological courses of study. In recent years seminary administrators have frequently approached Moscow's Russian-American Institute, modeled on liberal arts programs in U.S. Christian colleges, seeking advice on the formulation of a liberal arts curriculum. Perhaps the institution with the most successful expansion beyond theological studies in the former Soviet Union has occurred at Zaoksky Adventist University. Housed in, arguably, the most impressive, non-Orthodox campus in Russia, Zaoksky offers degrees in theology, music, English, social work, economics, accounting, law, public health, and agriculture.[75] Whatever one thinks of Adventist theology, this institution deserves close study for its commendable strides toward self sufficiency and for its exceptional breadth of program.[76]

One niche a Protestant seminary might consider would be studies in Orthodoxy from an evangelical perspective. Perhaps such an undertaking could be developed in tandem with Orthodox institutions open to working with Protestants such as St. Andrew's Biblical Theological Institute headed by Andrei Bodrov and the Orthodox Research Institute of Missiology, Ecumenism, and New Religious Movements headed by Father Vladimir Fedorov.[77] One would hope that such a program would attract a critical mass of faculty and students intent on realizing two readily justifiable goals for seminary education, as articulated by Estonian theologian Toivo Pilli: "to facilitate contextually relevant theological thinking and work in partnership with the churches" and to "interpret social, political, and religious changes in…society."[78] If Protestant seminaries should disappear in droves, one explanation could be their failure to discern the times, as Pilli urges.

Strengthening Church-School Ties

Of course, to survive, seminaries must strengthen ties with the churches in which they hope to place graduates.[79] As far back as an E-AAA conference in 1998 theological educators were recommending correctives to the school-church divide. Alexander Karnaukh (Odessa Baptist Theological Seminary) urged seminary professors to find teaching opportunities in churches. For his part, Rudolfo Giroi (Euro-Asian Theological Seminary of the Church of God Cleveland), at the same meeting, suggested "that students return to their churches in the middle of the [seminary] program."[80] In his thought-provoking dissertation on Protestant theological education in Central Asia, Insur Shamgunov warned that without close, vital links between school and church, "not only will the quality of training continue to suffer, but the very existence of the institutions will be in question."[81]

Taras Dyatlik's survey of 70 pastors from Ukraine and southern Russia seconds the concerns and advice of Karnaukh, Giroi, and Shamgunov. To foster closer church-school ties those surveyed recommended seminary prayer leaflet mailings (not email) and local pastoral representation on admission and graduation committees to assist in discerning "true motives and objectives of applicants" and to award diplomas "based in part on students' participation in church life and ministry during their theological training."[82] Over and over, pastors urged that students be required to "engage in practical education" back in their home churches during their formal studies. Maintaining such close ties might also forestall a seminary in a big city serving "as a kind of ski jump" enticing rural students to relocate in urban centers.[83]

Pastors surveyed also recognized that instructors actively involved in local ministry would more likely produce graduates aspiring to local ministry. The reverse, "cubbyhole professors" begetting "cubbyhole graduates of theology" would not nourish the church nor close church-school ties.[84] Pastors surveyed stressed the importance of "the spiritual lives of professors" for the successful mentoring of students:

> Regardless of the subject area in which professors teach, it is expected that their first priority should be to help their students become more mature Christians; providing them with academic knowledge should be second in priority.[85]

Taras Dyatlik believes schools that take these pastoral concerns to heart can expect growing local church support.[86]

Overcoming Western Dependency

To deepen the bonds between seminaries and churches, schools will have to decrease their dependence upon Western funding. To that end, enthusiastically or not, seminary administrators are having to become increasingly entrepreneurial because budgets have to start balancing. This is beginning to mean, and increasingly will mean, some combination of administrative and faculty cuts; sharing faculty with other institutions; charging students "meaningful" tuition;[87] selling some buildings; and leasing some space.[88]

More and more seminaries are designating space or retrofitting facilities to generate income from all manner of undertakings: an auto repair workshop (Donetsk),[89] weddings (St. Petersburg Christian University),[90] dorm rentals for tourists (SPCU), and hotel and conference centers (DCU, International Baptist Theological Seminary, and SPCU).[91] Donetsk, as an example, has hosted revenue-generating conferences for InterVarsity Christian Fellowship, the New Horizons English program, Eastern-Rite Catholics, and the East European Summit for Children at Risk.[92] In the past, seminaries sometimes turned down Western offers to help establish profit-making enterprises to help underwrite expenses—but no more. Donetsk raises its own vegetables and at Zaoksky students not only grow the food served in their cafeteria, they can vegetables and fruits and help staff a printing operation on campus.[93]

In addition to creative uses of campus facilities, seminaries must teach stewardship and must teach churches to teach stewardship.[94] Sadly, congregational offerings capable of underwriting significant church outreach run counter to practice in the evangelical subculture in the former Soviet Union. Many times one hears that Christians in post-Soviet lands are too poor to support their churches, much less seminaries. It is true that decades of Soviet persecution and discrimination meant minimal education and low-paying, menial labor for most believers. But Christians in Slavic lands are not the world's poorest. Many believers in the global South who contend with economic plights as bad as or worse than those of the former Soviet Union, support churches and sometimes even seminaries without the level of Western support that frequently pertains to the post-Soviet context. Theological educator Dieumeme Noelliste, as a native of Haiti no stranger to poverty, nevertheless decries the curse of Western dependence. The way out, he argues, is to follow Old and New Testament examples.

> The Scriptures make it clear that unfavorable socio-economic conditions are not necessary impediments to giving. Ancient Israel supplies an instructive example in this regard. While on the road to Canaan, the nomadic people built a splendid sanctuary to Yahweh with their own resources (Exodus 24-40). The "fundraising" drive that was conducted for that project brought in much more than was actually needed for the work. The biblical author took pain to emphasize that the success was not due to the people's abundant wealth, but to the willingness of their hearts (Exodus 35:20, 26, 29.)
>
> If we turn to the New Testament, we find similar examples. It is indisputable that, in the main, the early Christians were not well-to-do. In fact in I Corinthians 1:26, Paul candidly reminded Corinthian believers of their low status when they came to Christ. Yet, this did not prevent him from challenging them to participate fully in the support of the Lord's work—whether relief for the poor, the missionary campaign, or his own support (II Corinthians 8:1-15; Philippians 4:10-20). Nor did Christians themselves use their plight to claim exemption from responding to the apostle's appeal. Indeed, some of those poor believers stunned Paul by their generous response. Out of the Macedonians' severe trial and extreme poverty came a rich generosity that far exceeded their economic ability (II Corinthians 8:1-5).[95]

Expansion of Non-Formal Training Programs

As noted, the most concerted response to falling full-time residential enrollment has been the expansion of non-formal programs. Nomenclature in this arena can be confusing, so some definitions are in order.

1. An extension program typically caters to part-time students at a location some distance from a main campus, with adjunct faculty or faculty from a main campus.

2. A correspondence program typically provides instruction for part-time students some distance from a main campus via postal correspondence, and more recently, via the Internet.

3. An online program facilitates the instruction of students, usually part-time, but sometimes fulltime, typically some distance from a main campus, but not necessarily, via the Internet.

4. Distance learning encompasses all the above, except main campus online courses.

5. Non-formal and extramural education encompasses all of the above including main campus online programs. It may employ a non-traditional schedule (evenings or weekends) and/or a non-traditional calendar (typically one- to five-week modular courses, rather than lengthier quarters or semesters.)

Even with a clarification of terms, confusion still often persists because the lines between various forms of educational "delivery" frequently blur. The history of Protestant theological education in the Soviet Union illustrates the point. After the closure of their last Bible school in 1929, Protestants for many decades had no choice but to rely upon clergy mentoring of aspiring pastors, an unmistakable example of non-formal education. Then beginning in 1968 Soviet authorities grudgingly conceded a correspondence program to the only recognized nationwide Protestant denomination, Evangelical Christians-Baptists (ECB). Pastors enrolled in correspondence courses were permitted to travel to Moscow and Tallinn for brief period of fellowship and instruction. Over the years the length and importance of the on-site intervals steadily increased, so that by the end of the Soviet era, the on-site modules of correspondence programs had taken on much of the coloration of traditional residential seminary programs.[96] As another example today, students, East and West, increasingly mix and match components of traditional and non-formal education.

With definitions in mind, the next point to stress, as the ECB example underscores, is that non-formal theological education is nothing new in the Slavic context. It is being expanded, not invented, in response to the residential enrollment crisis. Another precedent was the consortium of visionary East European missions (Campus Crusade, Navigators, InterVarsity, and Slavic Gospel Association) that in 1979 launched Biblical Education by Extension (BEE), now known as Entrust, to provide pastoral training in Soviet-bloc countries.[97] In the last decades of the Soviet era sometimes even individual networkers managed to connect Western theological educators with churches desiring pastoral training, including Trevor Harris (SGA- United Kingdom) in Romania; Coach Don Church (Wheaton College) in Romania and Czechoslovakia; and Mark R. Elliott (Asbury College) in Estonia.[98] These Western extension efforts were well received because in the Soviet Bloc formal theological education for the vast majority of pastors was impossible.

Elusive Statistics

In the Soviet and post-Soviet cases reliable enrollment figures can be elusive. Nevertheless, as incomplete and debatable as statistics may be, they do underscore two indisputable points: 1) non-traditional theological instruction has long been significant; and 2) non-traditional programs and students account for the majority of pastors in training.

In 1992 the Orthodox Theological Seminary in Kyiv had 335 non-traditional students, compared to 214 full-time residential students. In 1993 Seventh-day Adventists instructed 500 extension course students at three sites.[99] In 1994 some 19 Protestant theological programs in the former Soviet Union enrolled 1,667 residential and 3,184 extension students.[100] In 1995 the Greek Catholic Theological Institute in Ivano-Frankivs'k, Ukraine, enrolled 800 extramural students compared to 480 full-time residential students.[101] In 2001 residential enrollment in 103 Protestant programs in the former Soviet Union (for which Overseas Council had data) totaled 9,789 versus 10,865 extension students.[102] As of 2004, St. Tikhon's Orthodox Theological Institute in Moscow, with a main campus and 13 branch sites, counted "up to 2,000 correspondence students."[103] By 2005 in the former Soviet Union the Russian Orthodox Church enrolled 5,700 correspondence students, compared to 5,155 full-time residential students.[104] And in 2009-10, seven Protestant training programs sponsored by Slavic Gospel Association in six post-Soviet republics enrolled 65 fulltime (presumably residential) students, compared to 921 part time students.[105]

For all practical purposes the Moscow Evangelical Christian-Baptist Theological Seminary (MTS) no longer operates a full-time residential program, while eight extension sites and online instruction account for 600 students.[106] The enrollment crisis became so acute at MTS that the school's trustees recruited consultants from the Euro-Asian Accrediting Association (Sergei Sannikov, Peter Penner, and Charley Warner) to offer advice. The outcome was the appointment of ECB Russian Union Vice-President Peter Mitskevich as rector in 2007, followed by a radical shift in emphasis from residential to extension training.[107] A major boost in non-traditional MTS enrollment came in late 2009 with its incorporation of Bible Mission International (Frankfurt, Germany, and Wichita, Kansas), with another 700 Russian-language correspondence students.[108] Moscow Theological Institute (MTI), affiliated with the Assemblies of God, presently enrolls 700 extension and correspondence students. MTI also anticipates a significant increase in its nontraditional program following a request in 2009 from 22 unregistered Pentecostal bishops and senior pastors for four new extension sites to provide training for unregistered pastors.[109]

Beyond denominational and mission-sponsored non-formal programs already noted, many other evangelical leadership training efforts serve additional thousands of students. With 750 enrolled, Training Christians for Ministry International (TCMI), based in Austria, probably has the largest number of Protestant correspondence students taking a master's level seminary course of study.[110] School Without Walls, organized by Peter Deyneka Russian Ministries (Association for Spiritual Renewal in the former Soviet Union), is providing pastoral extension courses in 62 sites in 49 regions reaching 1,813 students in 2008-09.[111] Peter Penner, who recently moved from the International Baptist Theological Seminary (Prague) to TCMI, and Jason Ferenczi (Overseas Council) give School Without Walls positive commendation.[112] Additional non-formal evangelical programs include East-West Ministries, READ, Precept Ministries, Bibel Mission, Leadership Resources International, BEE World, Church Leadership Development International, American Baptist International Ministries, International Theological Education Ministries (ITEM), and Theologians without Borders.[113]

Formal/Non-Formal Training Pros and Cons

As regards a comparison of residential and non-formal theological education, the advantages appear to be in many respects the same in the former Soviet Union as in any other part of the world. Residential programs provide a Christian witness of presence and visibility that nonformal programs lack.[114] In an historically Orthodox culture that places a premium on physicality in worship and majesty in architecture, visual presence and substantial construction cannot be discounted. Residential programs also offer the promise of spiritual formation in community that non-formal instruction cannot match. In addition, learning is enhanced when students can reflect and dialogue face-to-face with faculty and fellow students in hallways, cafeterias, and dorm rooms, as well as in classrooms. Finally, research on practical as well as academic topics is obviously facilitated with proximity to library resources.

In its favor, non-formal theological education, decentralized through extension centers, is typically closer to local churches than residential programs. Most pastors surveyed by Taras Dyatlik believe non-formal part time instruction works best "for the maintenance of students' relationships with local churches and their ministry."[115] Frequently it also is more practical in content and more flexible in finding ways to accommodate the needs and schedules of those already in ministry. In spirit and in fact, non-formal training is better situated than residential seminaries to avoid ivory tower isolation.

David Bohn and Miriam Charter, both with firsthand BEE experience, coincidentally completed Ph.D. dissertations the same year (1997) at Trinity Evangelical Divinity School, Deerfield, Illinois. Not coincidentally, under the guidance of their mentor, non-formal education advocate Ted Ward, both examined theological education in various post-Soviet countries, seeing greater promise in non-formal than in residential programs.[116] More recently, theological educator Toivo Pilli from Estonia has noted that church-based leadership training fosters "closer cooperation with churches, listening to their concerns and positions."[117] Foundation officer and adjunct professor David Sveen has documented the success of Josiah Venture's non-formal Leadership Internship Program in the Czech Republic and Slovakia.[118] For his part Ovidiu Cristian Chivu surveyed eight formal and non-formal training programs in Romania in his 2007 dissertation, concluding with his own proposal for church-based leadership training.[119]

Non-formal education, for all its merits, still has its detractors. One group of Central Asian seminarians surveyed by Insur Shamgunov noted that their non-formal program "placed a significant level of responsibility on the learner, which is simply not to be taken for granted." In the end, "many students dropped out of the course because they did not have enough diligence and skills for independent study."[120] In addition to low retention rates, non-formal programs are lengthier than formal programs (contributing to a higher dropout rate), less often lead to recognized degrees, and, especially in correspondence and online formats, lack adequate means of verification of students' work.[121]

The Need for Both Formal and Non-Formal Training

The contrasts between formal and non-formal theological education, however, need not, and should not, be drawn too sharply. In fact, as noted, many schools, for some time have provided both. As well, facing sparse residential enrollment, faculty in formal programs will increasingly staff still-growing, non-formal programs. In Romania, Danut Manastireanu bemoaned BEE and residential seminaries running "parallel courses with little cross fertilization."[122] In the former Soviet Union, by contrast, every residential school with an interest in surviving is launching or expanding some combination of extension, correspondence, and online delivery. As missionary Donald Marsden advised in 2006, "Theological educators in large cities, such as Moscow, St. Petersburg, Kyiv, and Odessa, need to consider how they can be a part of the training process for those in isolated provincial and rural regions who desire further training. High quality theological education needs to be delivered far and wide where potential students are currently active in ministry."[123]

Revising the Curriculum

It could happen that Protestant non-formal leadership training programs in the former Soviet Union will eclipse full-time residential theological education. However, if residential programs do survive, they will require a thorough reworking of the traditional curriculum. Metropolitan Hilarion has said the same for Orthodox seminaries: "Radical reform…is essential." For a start, teaching methods require attention. "We need a new approach to certain aspects of the *educational process*," the metropolitan urges. "Certain educational methods [such as slavish mimicking of 19th century homiletic style and content] we need to get rid of as soon as possible."[124] Insur Shamgunov and Mark Harris both believe mentoring should be as central to Protestant programs as classroom work.[125] Shamgunov's survey of graduates found that seminarians favored role models who are "wiser, older experienced ministers, not their own peers who finished seminary only a few years before" who "cannot offer much practical wisdom."[126]

In place of the traditional lecture format, Shamgunov advocates problem-based learning (PBL): Schools "could integrate the academic element of theological study with the development of students' skills in exegeting biblical texts, research, and preaching."[127] Shamgunov also stresses that theological training must constantly adapt to ever-changing political, religious, and economic conditions. While he has Central Asia in mind, flexibility would seem to be a prudent posture for seminaries throughout the former Soviet Union.[128]

In calls for curricular reform, two tendencies emerge: 1) the favoring of courses with practical, ministry application; and 2) the favoring of courses that can motivate and equip students to contribute to the transformation of culture, as well as congregations. The 2007 Overseas Council study revealed that, at least in the minds of graduates surveyed, the least important subjects in their curriculum were systematic theology, Hebrew, philosophy, radio production, Greek, and Ukrainian history (32 to 21 percent). In contrast, graduates ranked as most important for their ministry hermeneutics, introduction to the New and Old Testaments, church history, apologetics, spiritual counseling, evangelism and discipleship, and Christian ethics (91 to 81 percent).[129] In the majority of cases, courses with immediate practical ministry application scored highest.

Shamgunov rejects the traditional "fourfold divisions of biblical studies, systematic theology, church history, and practical theology," seeing this framing of the curriculum as the "fragmented formula of a theological encyclopedia." Instead, what is needed, he contends, is "a more holistic model, centered on the actual ministry of the church."[130] For Shamgunov courses serving this purpose should include social work, "counseling, social psychology, leadership, management, organizational development, strategic planning, time management, financial planning, and starting a business."[131] Vladimir Fedorov notes that some 19th century Russian Orthodox seminaries, for all their shortcomings, justifiably offered such utilitarian courses as medicine and bee keeping. For today's Orthodox seminarians he recommends missiology, psychology, cultural studies, political science, finance, law, and ministry to drug addicts and HIV/AIDS patients.[132]

While the courses Shamgunov recommends are all utilitarian, they aim at reshaping culture as much as serving local congregations. Caribbean theologian Dieumeme Noelliste dreams of a theological curriculum which boldly transforms culture, allowing graduates "to straddle both church and world." Courses must equip graduates with both "sound spiritual leadership" and a passion to deliver folk "from their fatalistic attitudes to take actions to alter their conditions." The curriculum, then, must hone "skills in community mobilization, community organization, community development, and the ability to speak prophetically to the context with the view to steering in the direction of God's ideal for societal life."[133] Similarly, Balkan Pentecostal theologian Peter Kuzmiè argues that if seminary graduates are to engage the culture they will need courses in psychology, philosophy, and sociology.[134]

Given the Slavic context, former missionary Donald Marsden urges course work in Orthodoxy, without which Evangelicals will be "doomed to a kind of intellectual vacuum in their own culture."[135] It is striking that Metropolitan Hilarion offers essentially identical advice in reverse—Orthodox seminarians should study non-Orthodox traditions.

> In my view, representatives of other confessions should be invited to meet with students and answer their questions. Someone may say, 'How can it be that a Protestant pastor or a Baptist preacher will come to an Orthodox theological seminary?' But then, in real life, our clergymen have to meet both with Protestant pastors and with Baptist preachers. Wouldn't it be sensible to prepare them for such meetings well in advance?

> Orthodox schools, the metropolitan contends, should educate in a spirit of tolerance and openness towards other confessions. We are now living not in the Middle Ages and not even in the nineteenth century. It should be born in mind that many of the future clergymen of our Churches will have to live in a multi-confessional society. They will have to be able not only to see the differences, but also to clearly understand that Christians belonging to most varied denominations have a single dogmatic basis, common belief in the Holy Trinity, belief in Jesus Christ as God and Savior.[136]

Courses in Counseling

As noted, Metropolitan Hilarion and a host of others recommend counseling and psychology for the seminary curriculum.[137] These subjects would serve good purpose based on needs in Central Asia. Pastors in this region surveyed by Insur Shamgunov convinced him that wounded hearts were commonplace in Central Asian churches and in the wider culture which had been "morally destroyed" in the Soviet era. Graduates face "alcoholism, drug abuse, occult practices, a high divorce rate, high unemployment, prostitution, and widespread domestic physical and sexual abuse!" Pastor Gulnora put it thus: "There is so much rejection in our society—women are rejected by men, children by their parents. People were much wounded during Soviet times; but nowadays children are rejected because parents are busy making money."[138]

The case for courses in pastoral counseling comes through clearly as well from the heart cry of a Lutheran pastor from Kazakhstan, put off by lengthy conference debates on academic qualifications for clergy. What is desperately needed, he argued, is "concentrated training in the basics for 'emergency preachers.'"

> I am in full agreement with much of the programs that you have presented here. But much that was said by American and European specialists cannot be connected with the concrete, burning needs of the churches and the believers, such as ours in Kazakhstan. We too allow ourselves to dream sometimes about grand plans, as they were developed at this conference. But in all honesty, they are for us at present quite unreal futurism. We face a mountain of problems: We are surrounded by people who feel lost, who seek comfort, intimacy, calm and a way to God. They are hungry abandoned children, lonely pensioners without means, mothers ready to give up the daily struggle for bread, drug addicted youth, young women who are forced to turn to prostitution to survive, and disoriented hopeless intellectuals. The church may not pass over them carelessly.[139]

Contextualization

The impassioned plea of this Lutheran pastor was that pastoral preparation take into account actual, contemporary social conditions as they exist in Kazakhstan. In other words, he was urging that the curriculum be contextualized. In the early 1990s, in the first panic to patch programs together posthaste, new Protestant seminaries emerged in the former Soviet Union that took little account of the social and cultural setting. "Western training programs were simply imported and installed."[140] Course texts were mostly translations from English; faculty, of necessity, to start with, were Western, Korean, or Western-trained; course offerings replicated those of schools abroad; and early on, even some seminary libraries held more English than Russian titles.[141]

A West-Knows-Best Mentality

Professor Ted Ward outlines sobering cautions for North Americans involved in theological training abroad. One "very dangerous and costly assumption," he warns, is the "longstanding habit in the Western world to assume that what *we* like to hear or see, *others* will like to hear or see.... What is good for us will be good for *them*."[142] Sad to say, too many Protestant programs, launched, led, and funded by Americans, labored under the handicap of an ethnocentrism that "tended to assume that proper training would help the Russian to think like an American."[143] Too often differences between Western and Slavic mentalities were not sufficiently taken into account.

Underscoring the East-West cultural divide, social scientist Geert Hofstede ranked Americans as the most individualistic of some 40 world cultures surveyed, whereas in his study Russians were among the most collectivist, typically deferring to majority preferences and traditions over personal wishes.[144] Unquestionably, some of the tensions in seminary classrooms have derived from divergent Western and Slavic mindsets. Examples include students hesitating to engage in class discussion or reticent to question a teacher imparting "received wisdom" and students "sharing" answers on a test for the good of the class average.[145]

St. Petersburg theological educator Sergei Nikolaev provides a startling illustration of an over-weaning, West-knows-best mentality among some seminary graduates:

> Recently I visited a church where a very interesting young man of wide reading, a graduate of a Russian theological institute was preaching. People were very attentive and listened to him with enthusiasm. In his sermon the young pastor quoted Spurgeon and Moody, Lewis and Berghoff, Stevenson and Barth, and I was carried away by his vast knowledge. But he did not even mention Solovyev or Bulgakov, Prokhanov or Florensky, Dostoevsky or Kargel.

How is it that he knows authors of foreign birth and does not know those of his motherland? Why does he think that Lewis and Barth have better answers to the hopes of his countrymen than do Solovyev and Alexander Men?[146]

Undoubtedly, this example underscores the need for theological education that is properly contextualized, taking into account Russian history, including one thousand years of Orthodox tradition.[147] Caribbean theological educator Dieumeme Noelliste calls for a creative synthesizing of Western and indigenous cultures, rather than a jealous, blind attachment to either exclusively: "What is needed is a critical appropriation of the legacy, involving the endorsement of its useful features, the adaptation of others, the correction of those deemed faulty, and the creation of new ones as may be required by the peculiarities of each environment."[148]

Of course, Nikolaev notes, "It is impossible to fruitfully serve your own people if you do not know your culture!" Still, he seconds Noelliste's call for the blending of the best of West and East: "To be able to communicate with people in comprehensible terms we have to find an effective way to combine the enormous experience of evangelical theology of the West with our native religious quest."[149]

Diverse developments, in fact, presently contribute to the contextualization of theological education in the former Soviet Union. The increase in national faculty with higher degrees is providing a major impetus to pastoral training appropriate to the context.[150] Also aiding the cause is a host of projects to identify, publish, reprint, and distribute books suitable for theological education: The Russian Protestant Theological Textbook Project; The Bible Pulpit Series of theological studies texts; the Euro-Asian Accrediting Association (http://e-aaa.info) with its conferences, school site visits, and CDs of historical materials; Theology Online (http://theologyonline.info), a consortium of Russian and Ukrainian schools facilitating interactive on-line instruction; the emergence of Christian publishers such as MIRT and Bibles for All; and the founding of Christian bookstores.[151]

As beneficial as contextualization can be, it bears noting that even the positive, taken to extremes, can sometimes prove harmful. For example, national and cultural pride can degenerate into chauvinism in some Ukrainian seminaries and churches as tensions flare over Russian versus

Ukrainian instruction and preaching.[152] Contextualization, then, cannot be allowed to serve as a cover for racially tinged nationalism which would trump the universality of the gospel and the common bond of love that sees "neither Greek nor Jew" (Galatians 3: 28).

In Summary

Protestant theological education currently faces serious challenges. Of course, in the Soviet era, state hostility led to many decades of no formal Protestant theological education at all. In contrast, the source of difficulties today stems primarily from an enrollment crisis[153] precipitated by a panoply of mostly self-inflicted wounds. Since the fall of Communism Protestant schools too often have overbuilt, have depended too heavily upon Western money and models, and have admitted too many marginal students. In addition, they too often have failed to maintain sufficiently close ties with the church, have adopted a more classical than practical curricula, and as a result, have produced graduates who frequently are ill-equipped for pastoral duties or are not welcome in the churches they have been trained to serve.

Consequences have included, and will continue to include, school closures and mergers, a more entrepreneurial approach to the use of facilities and faculty, and decreasing dependence upon Western direction and funding. Additional responses include increasing curricular revisions relevant to a Slavic context and diversification into liberal arts, business, and/or vocational degrees. Above all, schools are scrambling to develop or expand their nontraditional programs through correspondence courses, distance learning sites, and online instruction.

It is hoped that, ultimately, theological educators and their Western and indigenous stakeholders will come to realize that both traditional, residential theological education and nontraditional programs have their place and should be seen as complimentary.[154] Formal training typically has the advantage of spiritual formation in community, face-to-face faculty-student interaction, greater library resources, and campuses that provide a witness of presence and permanence. Informal training typically has the advantage of more practical content, more flexible schedules, and closer church-school ties.

To its detriment, formal training can lead to ivory tower isolation from the local church and less focused concentration on pastoral preparation. To its detriment, non-formal training typically is lengthier with less instructional oversight close at hand, has lower retention rates, provides less adequate verification of student work, and offers fewer recognized degrees. Thus, formal and nonformal programs have their strengths and weaknesses; both have their place; but both also require adaptation to the unique complexities of the post-Soviet environment.

Notes

1. Mark R. Elliott is editor of the *East-West Church & Ministry Report*, Asbury University, Wilmore, KY. A member of CAREE's Advisory Editorial Board for many years, Elliott presented this paper at CAREE's annual meeting in New York in February 2009, then up-dated it through use of sources as late as October 2010, making it a major review of the scholarship so far. Editor's note: Portions of this article were previously published in the *East-West Church & Ministry Report* 18 (Winter 2010), 16, 14-15; 18 (Spring 2010), 5-7; and 18 (Summer 2010), 13-15.

2. Matt Miller, email to author, 29 November 2009.

3. William Yoder, "The Future of Theological Education in Euro-Asia," news release, Department for External Church Relations of Russian Union of Evangelical Christians-Baptists, 22 August 2009; Ekaterina Smyslova, meeting, 5 December 2009; Gennady Sergienko, meeting, 26 May 2010.

4. Walter Sawatsky, "Reflections on the Urgency of Theological Education in the Former Soviet Union—After 20 Years," *Religion in Eastern Europe* 30 (May 2010), 25.

5. Jason Ferenczi, phone interview, 27 October 2009; Anthony Rybarczk, phone interview, 3 November 2009; Harold Brown, phone interview, 17 November 2009.

6. Insur Shamgunov, "Listening to the Voice of the Graduate: An Analysis of Professional Practice and Training for Ministry in Central Asia," Ph.D. dissertation, University of Oxford, 2009, pp. 19, 29, 34, and 36.

7. Mark R. Elliott, "Protestant Theological Education in the Former Soviet Union," *International Bulletin of Missionary Research* 18 (January 1994), 14; Mark R. Elliott, "Theological Education after Communism: The Mixed Blessing of Western Assistance," The Asbury Theological Journal 50 (Spring 1995), 67-73.

8. Alla Tikhonova, ed., *Spravochnik bogoslovskie uchebnye zavedeniya v stranakh SNG i Baltii* (Moscow: Assotsiatsiya Dukhovnoe Vozrozhdenie, 1999); Mark Elliott, "Theological Education in the Former Soviet Union: Some Recent Developments," *Religion in Eastern Europe* 21 (December 2001), 2.

9. Anthony Rybarczk, phone interview, 3 November 2009.

10. Yoder, "Future," 1.

11. David Hoehner, "Letter to the Editor," *East-West Church & Ministry Report* 15 (Winter 2007), 6.

12. Mark Harris, "Needed: A Revolution in Pastoral Training; Pitfalls of Western-Created Leadership Training in Russia," *International Journal of Frontier Missions* 20 (Fall 2003), 82. See also Taras Dyatlik, "What Expectations Do Pastors and Local Churches in the Former Soviet Union Have of Higher Theological Education at the

Beginning of the 21st Century?," *Bogoslovskie razmyshleniya/Theological Reflections* No. 10 (2009), 101, 103, and 115; Mark R. Elliott, "Protestant Missions in Russia Today," *East-West Church & Ministry Report* 13 (Fall 2005), 1; Ferenczi, "Theological Education," 7; Sawatsky, "Reflections,"22.

13. Peter Mitskevich, "Problems I See with Theological Education," *East-West Church & Ministry Report* 12 (Fall 2004), 6.

14. Wally C. Schoon, "The Lure of the West," *East-West Church & Ministry Report* 4 (Spring 1996), 1-2; Susan W. Hardwick, *Russian Refuge: Religion, Migration, and Settlement on the North American Pacific Rim* (Chicago: University of Chicago Press, 1993).

15. Shamgunov, "Listening," 23, 26, 29, 31, and 35; Jason Ferenczi, phone interview, 27 October 2009; Dyatlik, "Expectations," 115; Peter F. Penner, "Western Missionaries in Central and Eastern Europe," *Acta Missiologiae—Journal for Reflection on Missiological Issues and Mission Practice in Central and Eastern Europe* 1 (2008), 51.

16. Anthony Rybarcszk, phone interview, 3 November 2009; Jason Ferenczi, phone interview, 27 October 2009; Yoder, "Future,"2. Also, Polish Catholic seminary enrollments remain quite strong. Peter Penner and Anne Marie Kool, "Theological Education in Eastern and Central Europe" in *Handbook of Theological Education in World Christianity*, ed. by Dietrich Werner et al. (Oxford: Regnum Books International, 2010), 542.

17. Greg Nichols, email, 13 November 2009.

18. Harold Brown, phone interview, 17 November 2009, and Theological Education Conference, College Church, Wheaton, IL, 28 February 2008; Alexander Tsutserov, meeting, 27 May 2010; http://moscowseminary.ru/chart/chart/php.

19. Charley Warner, email, 27 October 2009. See also Harris, "Needed," 83.

20. Mitskevich, "Problems," 5-6; Harris, "Needed," 83; See also Sergei Golovin, "On Hopping Caterpillars, Spiritual Gastarbeiter, and Theological Education in Former Soviet Union Countries," 28 October 2009; http://www.scienceandapologetics.com/engl/g15.html; Mark R. Elliott, "Recent Research on Evangelical Theological Education in Post-Soviet Societies," *Religion in Eastern Europe* 19 (February 1999), 33 and 35; Dyatlik, "Expections,"107 and 109; Sawatsky, "Reflections," 24

21. Hieromonk Hilarion (Alfeyev), "The Problems Facing Orthodox Theological Education in Russia," *Sourozh, A Journal of Orthodox Life and Thought* 71 (1998), 3.

22. Mitskevich, "Problems," 5-6.

23. Dyatlik, "Expectations," 100.

24. Elliott, "Protestant Missions," 5.

25. Walter Sawatsky, phone interview, 26 October 2009. See also Sawatsky, "Reflections," 22 and 26.

26. Golovin, "Caterpillars." See also Mark R. Elliott, "Theological Education after Communism," 71.

27. Mitskevich, "Problems," 6. See also Elliott, "Recent Research," 35.

28. Jason Ferenczi, phone interview, 27 October 2009.

29. Mitskevich, "Problems," 6.

30. Metropolitan Hilarion Alveyev, "Theological Education in the 21st Century," http://en.hilarion.orthodoxia.org/print, p. 4.

31. Sergei Sannikov, ed., *The Effectiveness of Theological Education in Ukraine* (Odessa: Euro-Asian Accrediting Association, 2007), 78-79. See also Euro-Asian Accrediting Association, "The Effectiveness of Theological Education in Ukraine: A Research Project," *Bogoslovskie razmyshleniya/ Theological Reflections* No. 7 (2006), 149-205.

32. Shamgunov, "Protestant Theological Education in Central Asia: Embattled but Resilient," *East-West Church & Ministry Report* 17 (Fall 2009), 5.

33. *Ibid.*, 6.

34. Shamgunov, "Listening," 171-72, 211, 276, and 284.

35. *Ibid.*, 274.

36. *Ibid.*, 275.

37. Ibid., 25, 149-50, and 152; Elliott, "Protestant," 19; Cheryl and Wes Brown, "Progress and Challenge in Theological Education in Central and Eastern Europe," *Transformation* 20 (January 2003), 2; Jason Ferenczi, phone interview, 27 October 2009; I.P., email to author, 8 September 2005; Mark Harris, "Proposal for a Contextualized Educational Program for the Training of Russian Spiritual Leaders," www.markharris.us; Dyatlik, "Expectations," 103-04, 112, and 115.

38. Brown, "Progress," 2. See also Elliott, "Recent Research," 35; Donald Marsden, "Does Post-Soviet Theological Training Need to be Revamped?," *East-West Church & Ministry Report* 14 (Fall 2006), 1-3; and Dyatlik, "Expectations," 112.

39. Shamgunov, "Listening," 28, 150, and 286; Linda Eilers, "When Calvinist and Arminian Beliefs Collide: Facilitating Communication between North American Professors and Russian Bible Students," master's thesis, Trinity Evangelical Divinity School, 1998; Nicholas Holovaty, "A Moscow Case Study: Mixed Reviews for the Korean Pastor's School," *East-West Church & Ministry Report* 8 (Fall 2000), 8; and Sawatsky, "Reflections," 24.

40. Dyatlik, "Expectations," 102. See also *Ibid.*, 110-11 and 115.

41. Jason Ferenczi, "Theological Education," 12. See also Sawatsky, "Reflections," 116; Dyatlik, "Expectations," 117.

42. Ray Prigodich, meeting, 2 February 2008.

43. Ted Rodgers, phone interview, 26 October 2009; Elliott, "Recent Research," 32, quoting David P. Bohn, "A Comparative Study of the Perspectives of Evangelical Church Leaders in Bulgaria, Hungary, Romania and Russia on Theological Education," Ph.D. dissertation, Trinity Evangelical Divinity School, 1997, 193; Jason Ferenczi, phone interview, 27 October 2009; Dieumeme Noelliste, "Theological Education in the Context of Socio-Economic Deprivation," *Evangelical Review of Theology* (29 October 2005), 276.

44. Noelliste, "Theological Education," 282.

45. *Ibid.*, 276.

46. Hoehner, "Letter," 6.

47. Marsden, "Post-Soviet," 1-3. See also Penner, "Western Missionaries," 50; and Penner and Kool, "Theological Education," 541. A further disincentive for theological training is the fact that a seminary degree is not a requirement for ordination in Baptist and Pentecostal churches. Peter Sautov, meeting, 1 June 2010.

48. Turlac, "Crisis," 19; Dyatlik, "Expectations," 113.

49. Marsden, "Post-Soviet," 1-2; Jason Ferenczi, phone interview, 27 October 2009.

50. Marsden, "Post-Soviet," 2. See also Turlac, "Crisis," 19; and Dyatlik, "Expectations," 112.

51. Yoder, "Future," 2.

52. Turlac, "Crisis, 19.

53. Alister E. McGrath, *The Renewal of Anglicanism* (London: SPCK, 1994), 152.

54. Toivo Pilli, "Finding a Balance between Church and Academia: Baptist Theological Education in Estonia," *Religion in Eastern Europe* 26 (August 2006), 39-41.

55. Anne Marie Kool, "Leadership Issues in Central and Eastern Europe: Continuing Trends and Challenges in Mission and Mimssiology," *Acta Missiologiae* 1 (2008), 142.

60. Alexei Bodrov, "Mission and Theological Education in Contemporary Russia" in *Postmodernity-Friend or Foe? Communicating the Gospel to Postmodern People:*

Theological and Practical Reflections from Central and Eastern Europe, ed. by Alexander Neagoe and Heleen Zorgdrager (Utrecht: Kerk in Actie, 2009), 224-25. See also Sawatsky, "Reflections," 23.

61. Toivo Pilli, "Finding," 39.

62. Yoder, "Future," 1. See also Penner and Kool, "Theological Education," 541.

63. Yoder, 2; Brown, "Progress," 10-11; Noelliste, "Theological Education," 10-11; Dyatlik, "Expectations," 117; and Evgeni Bakhmutsky and Sharyl Corrado in Elliott, "Protestant Missions," 5.

64. Noelliste, "Theological Education," 10.

65. Gary Griffith, "New Bible Institute Registered in Bulgaria," *East-West Church & Ministry Report* 8 (Winter 2000), 14; Jason Ferenczi, email, 4 March 2010.

66. Yoder, "Future," 2.

67. Kool-Penner.

68. Jason Ferenczi, phone interview, 27 October 2009.

69. *Ibid*.

70. *Ibid*.

71. Shamgunov, "Listening," 249 and 278.

72. Noelliste, "Theological Education," 11.

73. Shamgunov, "Listening," 277.

74. Sawatsky, "Reflections," 24. See also Ferenczi, "Theological Education," 14-15.

75. Gary Land, *Historical Dictionary of Seventh-day Adventists* (Lanham, MD: Scarecrow Press, 2005), 336-37; "Zaoksky Adventist University," *Adventist Online Yearbook*, http://www.adventistyearbook.org.

76. Elliott, "Protestant," 16.

77. www.standrews.ru; http:///www.wcc-coe.org/wcc/what/interreligious/cd31-02.html. See also Dyatlik, "Expectations," 104.

78. Pilli, "Finding," 43 and 39.

79. Shamgunov, "Listening," 286-87; Turlac, "Crisis," 19.

80. Mitskevich, "Problems," 6. See also Elliott, "Recent Research," 35.

81. Shamgunov, "Listening," 286.

82. Dyatlik, "Expectations," 100, 107, and 113.

83. *Ibid.*, 109 and 111.

84. *Ibid.*, 114. See also Peter F. Penner, ed., *Theological Education as Mission* (Schwarzenfeld, Germany: Neufeld Verlag, 2005), 344.

85. Dyatlik, "Expectations," 113.

86. *Ibid.*, 117-18.

87. Jason Ferenczi, phone interview, 27 October 2009.

88. Ted Rodgers, phone interview, 26 October 2009.

89. Ray Prigodich, meeting, 27 February 2008.

90. Jason Ferenczi, phone interview, 27 October 2009.

91. Walter Sawatsky, phone interview, 26 October 2009.

92. Donetsk Christian University, On Campus Newsletter, Fall 2009, 2.

93. Elliott, "Protestant," 16; http://www.zau.ru.

94. Mark R. Elliott, "Post-Soviet Protestant Theological Education: Come of Age?," *The Asbury Theological Journal* 54 (Fall 1999), 38.

95. Noelliste, "Theological Education," 276-77.

96. Elliott, "Protestant," 14; Pilli, "Finding," 42-44.

97. Elliott, "Recent Research," 29. See also http://entrust4.org/423.ihtml.

98. Danut Manastireanu, "Western Assistance in Theological Training for Romanian Evangelicals since 1989," *East-West Church & Ministry Report* 14 (Summer 2006), 1-4; Mark Elliott, "Methodism in the Soviet Union Since World War II," *The Asbury Theological Journal* 46 (Spring 1991), 5-47.

99. Elliott, "Protestant," 22.

100. Ferenczi, "Theological Education," 2.

101. Jonathan Sutton, *Traditions in New Freedom: Christianity and Higher Education in Russia and Ukraine Today* (Nottingham: Bramcote Press, 1996), 92.

102. Ferenczi, "Theological Education," 3.

103. Wil Van Den Bercken, "Theological Education for Laypeople in Russia, Belarus' and Ukraine: A Survey of Orthodox and Catholic Institutions," *Religion, State and Society* 32 (September 2004), 300.

104. Vladimir Fedorov, "An Orthodox View on Theological Education as Mission," *Religion in Eastern Europe* 25 (August 2005), 25.

105. Slavic Gospel Association (Rockford, IL) sponsors Almaty Bible Institute, Kazakhstan; Baku Bible Institute, Azerbaijan; Irpen Biblical Seminary, Ukraine; Minsk Theological Seminary, Belarus; Novosibirsk Biblical Theological Seminary, Russia; Odessa Theological Seminary, Ukraine; and Tajikistan Bible Institute, Dushanbe. Full time students in the seven schools stood at 74 in 2007-08 and 55 in 2008-09 compared to 960 part time students in 2007-08 and 814 in 2008-09. Robert Provost, email, 4 February 2010.

106. Ted Rodgers, phone interview, 26 October 2009.

107. Ian Chapman, Theological Education Conference, 28 February 2008; Turlac, "Crisis," 19.

108. Ted Rodgers, phone interview, 26 October 2009; http://www.BibleMission.org.

109. Anthony Rybarczk, phone interview, 3 November 2009.

110. Peter Penner, email, 9 November 2009.

111. www.russian-ministries.org.

112. Peter Penner, email, 9 November 2009; Jason Ferenczi, phone interview, 27 October 2009.

113. Duane Elmer, Theological Education Conference, 28 February 2008; Bill Arvan, Theological Education Conference, 28 February 20008; Joe Wall, Theological Education Conference, 28 February 2008; http://www.eastwest.org; http://www.readministries.org; http://www.precept.org; http://www.russianleadership.org; http://www.bibel-mission.de/; http://www.leadershipresources.org; http://www.beeworld.org; http://www.cldi.org; http://www.internationalministries.org; http://christforrussia.org; http://theologianswithoutborders.blogspot.com.

114. Walter Sawatsky, phone interview, 26 October 2009.

115. Dyatlik, "Expectations," 104.

116. Bohn, "Comparative Study;" Miriam Charter, "Theological Education for New Protestant Churches of Russia: Indigenous Judgments on the Appropriateness of Educational Methods and Styles," Ph.D. dissertation, Trinity Evangelical Divinity School, 1997. See also Elliott, "Recent Research," 29 and 41; and Ferenczi, "Theological Education," 6-7.

117. Pilli, "Finding a Balance," 40.

118. David E. Sveen, "Leadership Development as a Non-formal Learning Experience in Central and Eastern Europe," Ph.D. dissertation, Trinity Evangelical Divinity School, 2004; and David E. Sveen with Mark R. Elliott, "Case Study of

Evangelical, Non-Formal Leadership Development," *East-West Church & Ministry Report* 16 (Spring 2008), 12-13.

119. Ovidiu Cristian Chivu, "Romanian Baptist Leadership Training," *East-West Church & Ministry Report* 17 (Spring 2009), 8-10; Ovidiu Cristian Chivu, "A Strategy for Church-Based Leadership Training in Romania," Ph.D. dissertation, Southern Baptist Theological Seminary, 2007.

120. Shamgunov, "Listening," 281. See also Ibid., 34.

121. Elliott, "Recent Research," 42; Walter Sawatsky, phone interview, 26 October 2009; Dyatlik, "Expectations," 105. MTS President Walter Mitskevich notes 83 MTS students enrolled in online training by the end of 2009. However, one quarter of students do not have their own computer and those in locations with under 100,000 residents lack reliable Internet access. Still, he observes, conditions are improving: "Russia is catching up." Mitskevich, email, 4 January 2010.

122. Danut Manastireanu, "Western Assistance: Theological Training for Romanian Evangelicals Since 1989," *East-West Church & Ministry Report* 15 (Winter 2007), 5.

123. Marsden, "Post-Soviet," 3. See also Nicholas Holovaty, "An Ideal Theological Education: The Vision of Moscow's Protestant Leaders," *East-West Church & Ministry Report* 8 (Fall 2000), 6.

124. Hilarion, "Problems," 1.

125. Harris, "Needed," 84; and Shamgunov, "Listening," 276 and 284.

126. Shamgunov "Listening," 284. See also *Ibid.*, 246-47.

127. *Ibid.*, 280. See also Toivo Pilli, "Toward a Holistic View of Theological Education" in *Theological Education as Mission*, ed. by Peter Penner (Hagen: Neufeld Verlag Schwarzenfeld, 2005).

128. Shamgunov, "Listening," 19 and 35. See also Harris, "Needed," 84.

129. Sannikov, Effectiveness, 75.

130. Shamgunov, "Listening," 279-80.

131. *Ibid.*, 30, 241, 257, 265, and 278. See also Tiberius Rata, "Theological Education in Romania," *East-West Church & Ministry Report* 10 (Spring 2002), 6.

132. Fedorov, "An Orthodox View," 30.

133. Noelliste, "Theological Education," 281-82. See also Pilli, *Dance or Die*, 116.

134. Elliott, "Recent Research," 3.

135. Marsden, "Post-Soviet, 3. See also Elliott, "Theological Education," 71; and Dyatlik, "Expectations," 104.

136. Hilarion, "Problems," 6.

137. *Ibid*. 7; Fedorov, "Orthodox View," 20; Shamgunov, "Listening," 241; Dennis Bowen and D. Russell Bishop, "Training Pastoral Counselors in Russia," *East-West Church & Ministry Report* 12 (Spring 2004), 3-5; Dennis Bowen, "Christian Counselor Training in Ukraine," *East-West Church & Ministry Report* 16 (Summer 2008), 4-6.

138. Shamgunov, "Listening," 7.

139. Gerd Stricker, "The Problems of Theological Education: The Experience of Lutheran Institutions in the CIS," *Religion in Eastern Europe* 21 (June 2001), 18.

140. Harris, "Needed," 84.

141. *Ibid.*; Elliott, "Theological Education," 69-71.

142. Ward, "Effective Development," 5.

143. Harris, "Needed," 84.

144. Geert Hofstede, "Cultural Differences in Teaching and Learning," *International Journal of Intercultural Relations* 10 (1986), 306-16.

145. Steve Chapman, "Collectivism in the Russian World View and Its Implications for Christian Ministry," *East-West Church & Ministry Report* 12 (Fall 1998), 12-14.

146. Sergei Nikolaev, "The Problems of Euro-Asian Theology for the New Millennium," *Religion in Eastern Europe* 20 (April 2000), 4.

147. Harris, "Needed," 84; Elliott, "Theological Education After Communism," 71.

148. Noelliste, "Theological Education," 278.

149. Nikolaev, "Problems," 4. See Shamgunov, "Listening," 274-75, for examples of Central Asian graduates successfully gleaning Christian texts from the West for their own purposes, rather than simply parroting them.

150. Ferenczi, "Theological Education," 13. Stricter visa regimes in Russia and Central Asia for visiting professors also underscore the necessity of national faculty. Mitskevich, email, 4 January 2010.

151. Ferenczi, "Theological Education," 8; Sawatsky, "Reflections," 25; Dyatlik, "Expectations," 105. St. Andrew's Biblical Theological Institute headed by Alexei Bodrov also sponsors the publication of many theological texts of value to Christians of all confessions. For a description of a wide range of Central and East European associations assisting indigenous theological education therefore contextualization, see Penner-Kool.

152. Yoder, "Future," 2; Nikolaev, "Problems," 3.

153. In a May 2010 meeting with the author in Russia, one Russian seminary president objected to the use of the term crisis to describe the current status of Protestant theological education, seeing his school's shift from a residential program to non-formal distance education as change rather than crisis. But the latter term has gained currency and is generally considered to be the state of affairs. This author first used the term and quoted indigenous sources using the term in print in 2005: Elliott, "Protestant Missions," 1 and 5. Western, Moldovan, and Ukrainian sources characterizing the state of Protestant theological education today as a crisis are: Sawatsky, "Reflections," 25; Turlac, "Crisis," 19; and Dyatlik, "Expectations," 97.

154. Ferenczi,"Theological Education," 7-8.

Communications Via Phone, E-mail, and Meetings

Arvan, William (READ) - 28 February 2008 meeting*;

Brown, Harold (OMS International) - 28 February 2008 meeting*; 17 November 2009 phone;

Chapman, Ian (Russian Leadership Ministries) - 28 February 2008 meeting*;

Ferenczi, Jason (Overseas Council International) - 28 February 2008 meeting*, 4 March 2009 email,

27 October 2009 phone, 4 March 2010 email;

I., P. (missionary in Ukraine) - 9 August 2005 email;

Mitskevich, Peter (Moscow Theological Seminary of Evangelical Christians-Baptists) - 4 January 2010 email;

Nichols, Greg (International Baptist Theological Seminary, Prague) - 14 November 2009 email;

Parushev, Parush (International Baptist Theological Seminary, Prague) - 14 November 2009 email;

Penner, Peter (TCMI, Vienna) - 9 November 2009 email;

Prigodich, Ray (The Evangelical Alliance Mission) - 27 February 2008 meeting;

Provost, Robert (Slavic Gospel Association, Elgin IL) - 4 February 2010 email;

Rodgers, Ted (Russian Leadership Ministries) - 26 October 2009 phone;

Rybarczk, Anthony (Assemblies of God) - 3 November 2009 phone;

Sautov, Peter (Russian Center for Church Multiplication) - 1 June 2010 meeting;

Sawatsky, Walter (Associated Mennonite Biblical Seminary) - 26 October 2009 phone;

Sergienko, Gennady (Second Baptist Church, Moscow) - 26 May 2010 meeting;

Smyslova, Ekaterina (Haggai Institute) - 6 December 2009 meeting;

Tsutserov, Alexander (Moscow Evangelical Christian Seminary) - 27 May 2010 meeting;

Wall, Joe (East-West Ministries) - 28 February 2008 meeting*;

Warner, Charley (Euro-Asian Accrediting Association, Vienna) - 27 October 2009 email.

* Theological Education Conference, College Church, Wheaton, IL, 28 February 2008

Chapter 10
Lessons from the Long-Shot Bid to Bring Christian Liberal-Arts Education to Russia
(2020)

In 1995, I taught a non-credit night course in Russian church history for what would become the Russian-American Christian University (RACU). It was a memorable experience on multiple counts. The class was held in rented space on the old campus of the Patrice Lumumba People's Friendship University, where a larger-than-life bust of the school's namesake Congolese communist martyr was on display in the lobby. Outside my classroom windows were the walls of the Donskoi Monastery, where the Bolsheviks imprisoned Russian Orthodox Patriarch Tikhon until his death in 1925. I team-taught in a stimulating partnership with a friend, Orthodox journalist and future priest Yakov Krotov. And I was teaching unusually attentive students as eager to learn as any I have ever encountered. For a few short years, less than two decades (1996-2011), an American-style Christian liberal arts university sought to plant seeds in Moscow, where the soil would grow increasingly rocky and thorny. Explanations for RACU's demise are easy to come by. They include an evangelical constituency limited in size and financial wherewithal, economic instability (including the 1998 ruble crisis and the 2008-09 recession), a political order devolving from pseudo-democracy to authoritarianism, deteriorating Russian-American relations, growing xenophobic nationalism, and a declining pool of college-age youth.

Above all, RACU could not overcome increasingly crippling state restrictions on private higher education and the lack of an established rule

---

Reprinted with permission from *Christianity Today Online*, 17 February 2020. https://www.christianitytoday.com/ct/2020/february-web-only/opening-red-door-john-bernbaum-russia-christian-liberal-art.html of law, which fueled (and was fueled by) pervasive corruption. Though the school was predominantly evangelical, it made earnest efforts to develop positive relations with the Russian Orthodox Church, efforts that were successful with some hierarchs but less so in the immediate neighborhood of its new building, which barely opened before pressures on all sides forced its closure and sale.

Fighting to Survive

Taking into account the overwhelming odds against RACU, a key question comes to mind: How did the school manage to survive as long as 17 years and produce ten graduating classes? Part of the explanation for its endurance lies in the enthusiastic support it received from elements of the U.S. Christian college network, as well as generous contributions from evangelical donors on and off its board. (Full disclosure: I was a member of that board.) But the chief reason for RACU's resilience was the competence and character of its founding president, John Bernbaum, who writes about his experience in *Opening the Red Door: The Inside Story of Russia's First Christian Liberal Arts University*.

Bernbaum's preparation for the post included a Ph.D. in European history, work in the U.S. State Department, decades of teaching and administrative experience with the Washington-based Council for Christian Colleges and Universities, and a gift for networking and donor development. Just as critical to the enterprise were Bernbaum's abiding sense of God's leading and a seemingly inexhaustible reservoir of energy, optimism, fortitude, and perseverance.

In the context of global Christianity, RACU was part of a rapid, multi-continent expansion of faith-based higher education over the past half-century—a phenomenon ably documented in the 2014 volume *Christian Higher Education: A Global Reconnaissance*. Compared to Asian and African newcomers, RACU's imprint was quite modest, at least quantitatively. With a student body that never exceeded 200, it was dwarfed, for example, by the 3,500 students of South Korea's Handong Global University (founded one year before RACU) or the 10,000 students of Nigeria's Bowen University (founded in 2002).

So why write an entire book on a school with such a limited lifespan and a quite modest enrollment? For one, the saga of RACU's hard-fought, short-lived existence bears telling because it played out in Russia, a nation that rightly commands the world's attention, for good or ill. In addition, RACU's promise and plight serves as a cautionary tale demonstrating the obstacles confronting any institution struggling to prevail in an environment of widespread corruption, economic uncertainty, and the arbitrary exercise of power.

Bernbaum's account features constant combat with corruption and bribery. Refusing to grease palms meant protracted, energy-sapping delays in obtaining an educational license, accreditation, and construction permits, to mention just the most obvious hurdles in Moscow's bureaucratic mazes. RACU gave witness to its ethical integrity through a persistent refusal to engage in the commonplace bribery that marked Russian higher education. The school never traded precious admission spots for favors. It never doctored test scores, final grades, or transcripts. And it never sold diplomas, although one enterprising fraudster did advertise a bogus RACU diploma for the equivalent of $500.

To date, it appears that RACU is one of only two Protestant higher education programs to have obtained Russian state accreditation (along with Zaokski Adventist University), a remarkable achievement given the partiality the state affords the Orthodox Church. Unfortunately, in 2009 the Ministry of Education abruptly changed a critical requirement for accreditation, ruling that doctorates issued by American universities were no longer valid in calculating the number of RACU faculty with higher degrees. This left the school with an albatross it could never shake.

Risk and Reward

Throughout its history, Russia has exhibited a love-hate relationship with the West, repeatedly alternating between periods of slavish imitation of Western ways and xenophobic rejection of all things foreign. The clash of Westernizers and Slavophiles in the 19th century is but one of many examples of this phenomenon. RACU was born during the fleeting ascendency of pro-Western, reform-minded, Yeltsin-era higher-education administrators. They were soon eclipsed by officials unsympathetic to private institutions, Protestants, and liberal-arts education. As a result, RACU's higher-education model—which stressed faith-based character formation and the creative stimulus of the liberal arts—has little purchase in Russia today. But that could well change if the country, in a post-Putin era, tamps down on nationalistic fervor and once again welcomes the influence of educational models from abroad. In its short existence, RACU's students came to appreciate the marketability of their new English-language and computer-science skills, but they also valued the school's spiritual stress on personal integrity, cross-cultural sensitivity, and lives lived for others. At some future date, the success of RACU's graduates could build momentum for a renewed experiment in a Christian liberal-arts education.

RACU's unsuccessful fight for long-term survival also serves as a case study for any institution determined to pursue a Christian mission in an unpredictable environment. To what extent should risk management inform decision-making? Was it prudent to invest so much time, effort, and money in a Christian university planted where the rule of law is lacking? Was it hopelessly naïve on the part of Bernbaum, his board, and his donors to paddle against the current? Certainly in rational, practical terms the odds against RACU were daunting. So to what extent are Christians to base their kingdom work upon rational, practical calculations?

For over a decade, I held a joint faculty-administrative appointment at a Christian college whose chief financial officer advised against short-term support for RACU, even as other Christian colleges with far smaller endowments proved willing to pitch in. I was told that the idea of a Christian college in Russia was too risky a venture. The irony is that this same American college never would have come into existence had its founder exercised a similar measure of caution and risk-aversion. To be sure, any Christian giving of consequence should involve the head and the heart alike, as Steve Corbett and Brian Fikkert argued so eloquently in their book *When Helping Hurts*. And it's no surprise that a financial officer, looking at all the relevant factors, would advise against investing in something as improbable as RACU. On the other hand, should the school's stakeholders be faulted for taking risks to fund a Christian liberal-arts university in such a strategic location? God willing, the day may come when forces of hope, liberty, and freedom of conscience regain ascendance in Russia. And in that day, something like the Russian-American Christian University, which performed so ably in its brief life, might flourish the way its founders intended.

Chapter 11
INCREASING STATE RESTRICTIONS ON RUSSIAN PROTESTANT SEMINARIES[1] (2020)

Introduction

Ivan Smirnov, I will call him, is originally from one of the western republics of the former Soviet Union, but presently studies in a provincial Russian Protestant seminary that authorities have attempted to close. Ivan believes it is providential his training has been able to continue: "Our God in His infinite grace has allowed our school to go on as an institution of higher education." So far, courts have ruled three times that the Russian Ministry of Education and Science "did not have any credible evidence which would give warrant to the state to shut us down." At one point the seminary's license was revoked but later reinstated, for which Ivan is thankful: "Praise the Lord for His mercy and protection!"

This young seminarian comes from a believing family: "My grandmother was threatened with drowning for her faith back in the early days of Communism." Later, "my father was not allowed to continue studies" even though he was an excellent student. Ivan relates he "chose to follow Christ at the age of 15," and since the end of Communist Party rule he has had the opportunity to openly serve in his church and pursue a theological education. He considers his life busy but blessed: "I am currently serving in the counseling ministry in my local church as well as preach and lead a small group." In seminary he has specialized in the study of the Old Testament and Hebrew, "so naturally the OT books of the Bible have had an impact on me."

Reprinted with permission from *Occasional Papers on Religion in Eastern Europe* 40 (No. 4, 2020): 1-31.

Ivan is aware of growing outside pressures on his church and his seminary: "There are some challenges from authorities in the life of the evangelical congregations...connected to the...[2016] anti-missionary [Yarovaya] law which has restricted the work of missionaries outside of the church premises." As for his seminary, to date the difficulties have been felt "mostly in the Academic Dean's office." Students carry on with their studies, although interspersed with periodic "updates about the current status of the legal process.... The vast majority of...students come motivated to gain proficiency and get equipped in a particular area of ministry. The question of a diploma (accreditation, licensure, etc.) is secondary."[2] Increasing state pressures upon Protestant seminaries to which "Ivan Smirnov" refers, is the subject of the present paper.

Summary of Statutes Affecting Protestant Seminaries

Russian Federation statutes applicable to the country's Protestant seminaries are of two types: 1) broad-stroke legislation that regulates church-state relations and non-governmental organizations (NGOs), and 2) laws regulating higher (tertiary) education. The first category includes the 1990 Law "On Freedom of Conscience," whose generous provisions were radically eviscerated in 1997 and 2016 legislation,[3] and the 2012 NGO Foreign Agent Law.[4] The second category includes a 1992 statute legalizing private higher education,[5] a 2004 presidential decree establishing the Federal Service for Supervision of Education and Science (Rosobrnadzor);[6] a 2008 law "On Changes...Concerning Licensing and Accreditation of Professional Religious Schools,"[7] and a 2012 Federal Law "On Education."[8]

Church-State and NGO Legislation

As regards church-state legislation, the 1990 Law On Freedom of Conscience made provision for religious expression to an extent never before realized in Russian history and rarely achieved by any state worldwide.[9] In the law's wake Russian Protestants, whose last Bible school Soviet authorities had closed in 1929, energetically, even frantically, launched numerous pastoral training programs with the help of coreligionists from abroad.[10] The number increased from a handful in 1992 to 71 in 1999. (For the entire former Soviet Union the number of Protestant theological institutions increased from approximately 40 in 1992 to 137 in 1999.)[11]

1997 Duma legislation "On Freedom of Conscience and Religious Associations Act," signed by President Boris Yeltsin, reversed the trend, introducing major impediments to the free exercise of religion.[12] However, two factors temporarily ameliorated some of the harshest restrictions imposed by this statute. First, uneven and sometimes haphazard enforcement was the rule in a state in which arbitrary administrative practice has always counted for more than the letter of the law. Second, Russia's Constitutional Court nullified some of the law's most repressive provisions.[13]

In contrast, 2016 legislation "On Combatting Terrorism" (No. 374-FZ), popularly known as the Yarovaya Law after the Duma deputy who introduced the bill, more aggressively infringes upon the rights of non-Orthodox religious adherents. Styled as an anti-terrorist measure, it in reality significantly curtails foreign and domestic missionary efforts very broadly defined and sharply undermines freedom of assembly and speech for all of Russia's non-Orthodox believers. President Vladimir Putin's much greater control over Russian courts, compared to Yeltsin, has also added teeth to Yarovaya restrictions upon minority faiths. In such a climate, Protestant seminaries were bound to suffer. According to one American respondent who previously taught in a Protestant seminary, the 2016 Yarovaya legislation had an immediate chilling effect upon widespread utilization of U.S. faculty in theological programs. Returning to Russia in early 2017, this individual was interrogated by an FSB agent for over an hour, one line of questioning centering on why Americans were needed as seminary instructors.[14]

Lastly, on the macro level, 2012 NGO legislation amounted to a fundamental assault on Russian civil society. Not surprisingly, branding private entities that receive financial support from abroad with the pejorative label of "foreign agent" led to the closure or reduced effectiveness of many Russian NGOs.[15] Religious bodies, including Protestant seminaries, which to this day receive Western and South Korean financial assistance, are exempt from the "foreign agent" moniker. Nevertheless, state-controlled media have crafted a hostile public perception of these pastoral training programs based in part on their ties abroad. As a result, they live in fear that their official status might yet be tarnished with the "foreign agent" brush.

Higher Education Legislation

A review of educational legislation affecting Protestant seminaries begins with the Duma's legalization of private higher education in 1992.[16] The number of such institutions subsequently increased in just over a decade from 78 in 1993-94 to 409 in 2004-05, while private higher education enrollment increased in the same years from 70,000 to over one million, or roughly 15 percent of total tertiary enrollment.[17]

For a host of reasons the state came to view this growth of private institutions as uncontrolled and problematic, as it also deemed the increase in the total number of higher educational programs, private and public, to 1,071 by 2007.[18] State responses have included the presidential decree of 2004 and legislation in 2008 and 2012 previously noted. Rosobrnadzor, the federal higher education regulatory agency established in 2004, found its authority greatly enhanced by means of the 2008 and 2012 statutes. Konstantin Petrenko and Perry Glanzer (Baylor University) note that "The centralized nature of Russian higher education and the influence that the Ministry of Education exerts over a school's curriculum would be surprising to anyone in the West."[19]

With Putin publicly mandating improved quality and increased competitiveness in higher education, Rosobrnadzor was charged with responsibility for close scrutiny of the performance of all post-secondary institutions.[20] By the 2015-16 school year the number of universities and institutes stood at 896, down 175 in a decade.[21] In 2014-17 alone Rosobrnadzor revoked 58 educational licenses, terminated the accreditation of 125 institutions, and ordered a halt to admissions in an additional 68 universities. Seventy of these programs reopened after correcting Rosobrnadzor citations, but the trajectory of tightened, potentially lethal oversight was clear.[22] In 2015 Minister of Education and Science Dmitry Livanov referred to the process as a "clean-up" of higher education. His goal was a 40 percent reduction in the number of public universities and an 80 percent reduction in their branch campuses.[23] The outcome has been the state's ongoing merger of "inefficient" universities and the closure, to date, of roughly half of all branch campuses.[24]

Livanov also specifically targeted non-public institutions: "We want to reduce private universities which provide low quality education."[25] Even before Livanov's tenure, his predecessor as Minister of Education and Science, Andrei Fursenko (2004-12), had publicly stated a goal of "a maximum 50 universities and 150 to 200 institutes of higher education."[26] Rector Gennadi Pshenichny of Kuban Evangelical Christian University deems a 2015 Rosobrnadzor "audit" of non-state schools as "in reality…a state-sanctioned lever to decrease the number of private institutions of higher learning and funnel the students into state-sponsored/state sanctioned schools."[27]

Factors Behind Increasing Oversight: Quality Control

In analyzing factors behind increasing state oversight of post-secondary education commentators frequently cite the need for greater quality control. This explanation is the case not only with Putin and the Russian Ministry of Education and Science, but even with some Protestant theological educators. Aleksandr Spichak, academic dean of the Protestant Trinity Video Seminary in Kursk, writes, "Many secular universities are closed down…because many of them were just selling diplomas, and the government does want to improve the quality of higher education and get rid of fake institutions."[28] Sergey Chervonenko, administrator at the interdenominational Moscow Evangelical Christian Seminary, notes, "In the period of the 90s, there was no order in the country.…There was no regulation of educational activities, so a great many educational institutions appeared that were distributing diplomas."[29]

The early post-Soviet period was indeed rife with for-profit as well as nonprofit programs of uneven quality, popularly characterized as "diploma mills."[30] Professor Olga Zaprometova, holder of two earned doctorates and former dean of the Pentecostal Eurasian Theological Seminary, has taught and currently teaches biblical studies at a number of Moscow's Protestant and Orthodox seminaries. Her opinion is that "the Lord is using these [Rosobrnadzor] visits to improve the educational level of Protestant seminaries." She adds that professors need to teach only in their fields of expertise, that faculty need to be engaged in professional growth and development, that administrators need assistance in honing their competencies, and that future pastors need instruction in proper command of the Russian language. When asked if increasing state oversight of higher education, including Protestant seminaries, was part of an overall government strategy to bring all sectors of Russian society under closer supervision, Zaprometova responded,

I am not so sure about it, but it is a wise strategy, because there is no supervision of the Christian schools by church officials (board members, etc.), plus quite often board members are not qualified enough for this ministry, they do not have higher education or got it recently, even online or from the same Christian school, there are almost no Ph.D.s among church supervisors, and without supervision, especially in the academy, the quality of Christian education is drastically going down![31]

Factors Behind Increasing Oversight: Demographics

In addition to improved quality as a motivation for audits, other factors appear to be at play behind Rosobrnadzor's strict accounting of higher education in general and Protestant seminaries in particular. First, demographics come to bear on the issue.[32] A 2005 estimate projected a Russian population decline from 144.1 million in 2004 to 50 to 100 million by 2050.[33] As this population shortfall relates to education, between 2000/01 and 2014/15 the number of secondary school graduates fell from 1.46 million to 701,400, with a resulting drop in tertiary enrollment from 7.5 million to 4.2 million students between 2008/09 and 2014/15.[34] The projected decrease in higher education enrollments— "by as much as 56 percent between 2008 and 2021"—undoubtedly contributes to state measures to reduce the number of institutions—and associated costs—of higher education.[35] Thus, cuts in tertiary education expenditures and school mergers and closures stem in part from budgetary pressures. Educational funding has also been compromised by falling tax revenues due to declining oil and gas prices and Western sanctions triggered by Russian annexation of Crimea and its military intervention in eastern Ukraine.[36]

One consequence of Russia's demographic decline is heightened competition for higher education enrollment and lobbying by public institutions to reduce competition from their private counterparts.[37] And as noted, the state has obliged by making life more difficult for non-public universities and institutes.

Factors Behind Increasing Oversight: The Predictable Goal of an Authoritarian State

In 2019-20 Protestant educators and leaders gave responses to the following survey question:

> Is increasing Russian state oversight of private educational institutions, including Protestant seminaries, a justifiable effort to standardize higher education and ensure quality [or] part of an overall government strategy to bring all sectors of Russian society under closer state supervision?[38]

Moscow Evangelical Christian Seminary's Sergey Chervonenko answered, "Rosobrnadzor checks, in my humble opinion, are part of a program aimed at strengthening control over education." Yet he views this oversight positively because thereby "Religious universities have the opportunity to stand on a par with state universities."[39] The leader of one Protestant denomination related a "tough but successful" Rosobrnadzor inspection of his church's seminary, but did not consider it to be discrimination against non-Orthodox. Rather, he viewed it as part of the "overall trend in all sectors of society to have more [state] control."[40] Similarly, but less positively, Roman Lunkin, a scholar of religion in the Russian Academy of Sciences, contends, "The Russian state's policy on religious education has become a mirror image of its sweeping control over all social initiatives and non-governmental organizations."[41]

Several personal observations are in order. First, it bears noting that authoritarianism has been a characteristic of the Russian state for centuries—under tsars, commissars, and now Putin. As regards Russian higher education today, sources are uniform in recognizing growing state involvement. Judging whether or not this increased oversight is for good or ill is where disagreements occur. Certainly, quality control has its place. However, augmented control does not necessarily guarantee quality. To the contrary, as coming case studies will attest, rigorous oversight can actually undermine quality through personal bias, arbitrariness, and corruption, faults greater controls ironically are meant to reduce.

One consequence of increasing supervision of higher education that the state, no doubt, finds especially useful is the greater ease it affords it in controlling the tertiary sector. Authoritarian rule in Russia has a longstanding penchant for consolidation for the sake of "efficiency." Two examples may illustrate the point. In 1944 Stalin required the merger of the Evangelical Christian and Baptist denominations to facilitate the streamlining of Kremlin directives to Protestants through a single, centralized administrative structure. Second, in 2007 Putin managed the improbable absorption of the Russian Orthodox Church Abroad (ROCA) into the Russian Orthodox Church Moscow Patriarchate, the very body that ROCA had anathematized for decades as a pawn of the Soviet state. It may be argued that Putin engineered this merger for much the same reason that Stalin created the Evangelical Christian-Baptist Union: for ease of control, in this latter case, to better coordinate the utilization of Russian Orthodox/Kremlin soft power abroad.

Factors Behind Increasing Oversight: Fighting Corruption

A commendable aspiration of Rosobrnadzor has been its fight against corruption in higher education. Transparency International's most recent Corruption Perceptions Index (2019) ranks Russia 137th out of 180 countries, a drop from its 131st place out of 176 countries in 2017.[42] Corruption has been a widely recognized feature of Russian life for centuries under both tsars and commissars. The tsarist era is replete with accounts depicting bribery and corruption as both corrosive and commonplace, including *Journey for Our Time* by French memoirist the Marquis de Custine (1839); *The History of a Town* (1870) and *The Golovlyov Family* (1876) by satirist Mikhail Saltykov-Shchedrin; and most famously, *The Inspector General* (1836) and *Dead Souls* (1842) by Nikolai Gogol. Study of the massive scale of extra-legal economic activity in the Soviet era is associated especially with the pioneering work of Gregory Grossman, beginning in the 1970s.[43] In the post-Soviet era, some argue, corruption has reached colossal proportions beyond anything ever before endured in Russia. Since 1991 the nation's assets have been plundered for private gain on a massive scale by a consortium of mafia, state officials, past and present security service operatives, and newly minted billionaire oligarchs.[44]

Corrupt practices in higher education, ubiquitous in the Soviet era, have continued unabated since the collapse of the Soviet Union.[45] Elizaveta Potapova, research fellow of the Institute of World Economy and International Relations of the Russian Academy of Sciences, notes that post-secondary education "is particularly vulnerable to corruption" because most faculty are poorly paid, and many students "are willing to pay instructors for better grades, revised transcripts, and more."[46] Gennadi Gudkov, head of a Duma Anti-Corruption Committee, estimates that the bill for corruption in higher education may total the equivalent of one billion dollars annually. In Moscow alone, this Duma committee asserts, "each year 30 to 40 professors are caught accepting bribes in exchange for grades."[47]

University admissions have been particularly susceptible to malpractice. Bribes to gain admittance to Moscow universities and institutes are estimated to have totaled $520 million USD in 2008 alone, with individual student under-the-table payments up to $5,000. In 2009 Rosobrnadzor made mandatory a nationwide standardized higher education admissions test aimed at eliminating fraud in the process, which did reduce direct bribes. However, corruption is said to continue through payments for covert distribution of test questions and post-exam correction of wrong answers.[48]

Other corrupt practices in higher education include the sale of diplomas and plagiarized and ghost-written papers and dissertations. Some studies suggest that since the collapse of the Soviet Union 30 to 50 percent of Russian doctoral degrees in law and medicine have been plagiarized and that 20 to 30 percent of dissertations have been "purchased on the black market."[49] In the same vein, "a 2015 study by the Dissernet Project, an organization dedicated to exposing academic fraud, found that one in nine politicians in the lower house of the Russian parliament had a plagiarized or fake academic degree."[50] A 2006 Brookings Institution study of Vladimir Putin's 1997 dissertation speaks to the pervasiveness of fraud that is seemingly endemic in Russian higher education. Brookings fellows Clifford Gaddy and Igor Danchenko determined that in Putin's dissertation "More than 16 pages worth of text [out of a nearly 20-page segment] were taken verbatim" from *Strategic Planning and Policy* by American economists William King and David Cleland. Even more disturbing than Putin's plagiarism is the fact that "The scandal…led nowhere."[51] Given these facts, is it possible for a plagiarist to succeed in superintending a significant upgrade in the quality of Russian higher education? More colloquially, can a fox guard a hen house?

Orthodox Advantages and Protestant Disadvantages

State dealings with Russian Orthodox seminaries, in comparison with Protestant seminaries, underscore the disadvantages the latter face. On the one hand, theological educator Zaprometova observes that Orthodox theological schools away from Moscow often face serious challenges from Rosobrnadzor. As a result, many Orthodox, as well as Protestant seminaries, have chosen not to seek state accreditation as too burdensome a process.[52] As theologian John Burgess, author of *Holy Rus; The Rebirth of Orthodoxy in the New Russia*, has put it, theological educators of diverse confessions dread the weight of "heavy-handed bureaucracy" that accreditation entails. Illustrating the "reality of a highly bureaucratized society," he notes that state authorities threatened Belgorod Orthodox Seminary with a fine for a minor infraction: its website was said not to be up-to-date.[53] On the other hand, Orthodox institutions in Moscow which have obtained state accreditation, such as St. Tikhon Orthodox Humanitarian University and the Russian Orthodox University of St. John the Theologian, have had no difficulty securing it, "probably due to their political connections and influence."[54]

Also to the advantage of the Orthodox church is the relative ease with which they obtain premises for instruction. The state, for example, has afforded St. Tikhon and St. John free or nearly free use of Moscow buildings that had been the property of the Orthodox Church before the 1917 Revolution. Rector John Ekonomtsev of St. John regretted how "very difficult" it was "to actually get a building free of charge." The Patriarch reportedly approached Putin personally to help secure St. John's building.[55] In contrast, Protestant seminaries have typically encountered protracted difficulties gaining permission to build, lease, or rent property at any cost. Protestant educators could only hope for the "troubles" Orthodox experience finding facilities. That government authorities called upon St. Tikhon University to write state standards for theological degrees, applicable to non-Orthodox, even Jewish and Islamic, as well as Orthodox institutions, is another indication of the Kremlin's favoring Orthodoxy.[56] As Russian Academy of Sciences scholar Roman Lunkin notes, "It is clear from…state religious policy trends that officials often understand protection of the Russian Orthodox Church as necessitating discrimination of other religious communities."[57]

It may be argued that the Russian Orthodox Church enjoys the de facto status of an established church. Patriarch Kyrill's frequent public appearances with President Putin and the panoply of legislative restrictions placed upon non-Orthodox faiths since 1997 form the context in which punitive state scrutiny of Protestant seminaries should be understood. In this author's 2019-20 survey of Protestant theological educators and church leaders, three options were posed as possible explanations for "increasing Russian state oversight of private educational institutions, including Protestant seminaries." Two of the three have been previously discussed: option one, "a justifiable effort to standardize higher education and ensure quality," and option two, "an overall government strategy to bring all sectors of Russian society under closer state supervision."

The third option offered to account for impediments facing Protestant seminaries is to view them as part of state measures to discriminate against, and in some cases suppress, non-Orthodox faiths, in keeping with the close collaboration between the state and the Russian Orthodox Church. In a sentence, ample evidence exists to conclude that all three factors contribute to the challenges faced by Protestant pastoral training programs.

This is not the place to enumerate the myriad ways in which Russian state policies marginalize and state-dominated media malign non-Orthodox faiths, despite formal constitutional protections for freedom of conscience for all. The Russian Constitution explicitly states, "Religious associations shall be separated from the State and shall be equal before the law."[58]

Just one facet of the uphill struggle faced by Russian Protestants should suffice to illustrate the point. Compared to the thousands of Russian Orthodox parishes now in possession of churches returned to them by the state, Protestants and other non-Orthodox confessions frequently struggle to secure and hold on to places of worship. Roman Lunkin notes that "local officials prefer not to apply the 2010 Law on Restitution of Property of Religious Significance to Religious Organizations to churches other than the Russian Orthodox Church." Examples abound. Old Believers have been denied the return of their church buildings in Kirov, St. Petersburg, Saratov, and their Dormition Church in Moscow. Similarly, Roman Catholics have been unable to retrieve Sts. Peter and Paul Church in Moscow, nor their previously confiscated sanctuaries in Barnaul, Belgorod, Blagoveshchensk, Chita, Kirov, Krasnoyarsk, and Smolensk. Most egregious, the state has turned over various non-Orthodox houses of worship to the Russian Orthodox Church: more than a dozen former Catholic and Lutheran churches were handed over to Orthodox in Kaliningrad, the former Prussian city of Konigsburg, and the same for a Catholic church in Belgorod. Lutherans have also unsuccessfully appealed for the return of churches in Krasnodar, Smolensk, Simferopol, Sudak, Yalta, and Evpatoria.[59]

In contrast, Protestants, other than Lutherans, have few historic properties that would be eligible for restitution, though two secularized Baptist sanctuaries in Kaliningrad and St. Petersburg should be candidates.[60] Instead, Protestant struggles for places to worship typically have involved the denial of building permits, Orthodox pressure on local owners to refuse or to revoke lease and rental agreements, and local officials prohibiting the use of private residences for worship.

It follows predictably that in this general climate of state partiality toward the Orthodox and discrimination against non-Orthodox, Protestant seminaries would suffer. Roman Lunkin well summarizes this point:

> Educational institutions founded by other [non-Orthodox] faiths and denominations—above all, Protestants—function under the pressure of constant inspections, and have even faced closure. The campaign against such institutions form a logical part of the state's policy of restricting non-Orthodox mission, banning worship services in private homes, and barring Protestant church construction. It would be strange, after all, if the authorities looked kindly upon Christians receiving higher theological education unimpeded, while at the same time placing fines on them and confiscating their property.[61]

Conflicting Views on the Applicability of Religious Versus Educational Legislation Upon Seminaries

The precise legislative basis for Rosobrnadzor audits and penalties imposed upon Protestant seminaries is a matter of debate. Reporter Victoria Arnold, in a detailed treatment of the subject for the freedom of conscience news service *Forum 18*, contends, "Religious educational institutions are under no obligation to acquire state accreditation, and many have operated for years without it, including the Baptist and Pentecostal seminaries discussed here, the Catholic Church's Mary, Queen of the Apostles Higher Seminary in St. Petersburg, and the Lutheran Church Seminary in Novosaratovka, near

St. Petersburg." Furthermore, Rosobrnadzor inspections are undertaken on the basis of "somewhat vague legislation [that] may be misapplied, e.g. in the two parallel systems of state-accredited and non-state-accredited religious educational institutions."[62]

Regarding 2018-19 audits of Moscow's Baptist and Pentecostal seminaries, Arnold wonders "why inspectors had treated the courses offered by these religious educational establishments as if they were state-accredited and therefore obliged to abide by state requirements, when according to the law...such institutions have the right to offer non-state-accredited programmes which must conform only to the standards of the responsible religious organization." The consequence, she argues, is "the possibility of disproportionate punishment for infractions which are minor or which institutions themselves insist they have not committed. Such punishments include suspension of admissions, suspension of activities, and revocation of licences–all of which arguably have a greater longer-term impact on an institution's functioning than a fine."[63]

In contrast to *Forum 18*'s interpretation, Russian authorities insist–and carry the day– that Protestant seminaries are subject to both 1997 legislation, "On Freedom of Conscience and Religious Associations" (125-FZ), as amended 19 times between 2000 and 2016,[64] and 2012 legislation, "On Education in the Russian Federation" (273-FZ). As Moscow Evangelical Christian Seminary President Sergei Chervonenko relates, 2018-19 Rosobrnadzor inspections focused on provisions of 2012 "On Education" legislative requirements, "practically without touching or gently circumventing everything related to 125-FZ [the 1997 Law On Freedom of Conscience]." Chervonenko continues, "In practice, it turned out that some religious universities [and seminaries] were not ready for such a development of events and emphasized their religious status." Nevertheless, "Those [seminaries] that insisted that they were not bound by the requirements of the 2012 law proved to be mistaken."[65]

A key mechanism for state (Rosobrnadzor) oversight of higher education is its authority to license and accredit.[66] A license permits an institution to conduct educational programs and to admit students, while accreditation allows an institution "to award nationally recognized degrees," to extend military deferments to students, and to afford graduates the right to seek employment in the government sector and to pursue graduate degrees in state-accredited universities.[67]

A series of 2008 Rosobrnadzor higher education inspections determined that many private sector programs, including many Protestant seminaries, were operating without a valid license, and as a result, were forced to close.[68] More recently, between January 2018 and March 2019, Rosobrnadzor conducted audits of 16 religious educational programs (two Russian Orthodox, three Muslim, three Baptist, two Pentecostal, one Adventist, and five additional Protestant). Inspectors recorded violations in all but one case.[69] Penalties ran the gamut: fines, suspended or revoked licenses, suspension of admissions, suspension of instruction, and revocation of accreditation. As Andrei Kortunov observed, "This dependency has been considered by the majority of the Russian educational community to be a liability, and all the history of the Russian higher education demonstrates continuous attempts of universities to achieve more autonomy from state bureaucrats."[70]

Victoria Arnold's *Forum 18* reporting devotes considerable space to the consequences of 2018-19 inspections upon three Protestant institutions–Moscow Theological Seminary of Evangelical Christians-Baptists (MTS), the Eurasian Theological Seminary of the Russian Pentecostal Union (ETS), and the interdenominational Moscow Evangelical Christian Seminary (MECS).

Moscow Theological Seminary of Evangelical Christians-Baptists

Moscow Theological Seminary (MTS) has been the leading pastoral training program of the Evangelical Christian-Baptist (ECB) Union. Successor to the correspondence course permitted by Soviet authorities beginning in 1968, its residential instruction commenced in 1993 in Moscow in the ECB headquarters on Varshavskoye Shosse, shifting in 2002 to its own facility in a renovated elementary school building. At the beginning of 2020 MTS was instructing some 375 students in Moscow and another 555 in eight additional distance learning centers across Russia.[71]

Following an October 2018 inspection, Rosobrnadzor cited MTS for "gross violation of the requirements and conditions of a special permit (license)," leading to a court case against the school on 18 October. The seminary submitted responses to Rosobrnadzor citations on 19 November and 28 December. Meanwhile, on 27 December Moscow's Perovo District Court found the seminary non-compliant and ordered a 60-day suspension of activities.[72]

In the midst of a follow-up inspection, 15-17 January 2020, a seminary appeal of the court decision failed. The suspension began on 25 January with the sealing of the building by bailiffs. On 15 February 2020 Rosobrnadzor also imposed a ban on new MTS admissions. Courts subsequently extended the suspension, including a prohibition on the use of the seminary building for any purpose. At this point the seminary reverted to a non-formal, non-credit instructional program back on the premises of the ECB headquarters building under conditions reminiscent of the semi-underground pastoral training of the Soviet era.

Most recently, on 27 February 2020, came word of a Moscow arbitration court's revocation of the MTS license. According to the seminary's stunned Vice-Rector for Academic Affairs Aleksei Markevich,

> The main complaint of a "violation" of licensing requirements was the "incorrect" form of a document describing the teaching load, although this form was developed in accordance with the law.... Revocation of a license is an extreme measure, which the government uses when an organization, by its activity, grossly violates the law and threatens society, the state, or citizens. Evidently the judge saw in our seminary such a threat. Many ask, what is the reason for such a decision. I see it as a carte blanche that is given to the Russian bureaucracy and the lack of independent judicial procedures. But that is my personal opinion, a person who has tried for a year and a half to do everything to satisfy this bureaucracy [Rosobrnadzor], which turned out to be impossible.

Two months prior, in December 2019, perhaps in anticipation of a worst-case scenario, Rector Peter Mitskevich had written in a communication to the entire ECB denomination, "We want to be obedient to God here. It is all in His hands. We will train people to be gospel servants whether it is unofficial in the church, or in an official seminary context."[73]

Mitskevich, who has served as rector of MTS since 2007 and as president of the ECB Union since 2017, has clearly been laboring under a formidable administrative burden.[74] His heavy workload, which also includes pastoring Moscow's Golgotha ECB Church since 2004, means he may not always have been able to give sufficient attention to documentation that a highly bureaucratic Russian administration requires and that a truly fulltime rector would have been able to oversee. In addition, Roman Lunkin suggests, "Rosobrnadzor bureaucrats expect documentation to be drawn up by the experts they have recommended. Protestant institutions like the Moscow Baptist Seminary insist on their independence, however, and thus have ended up adopting a confrontational approach."[75]

To have survived intact in its bouts with the Ministry of Education and Science, Lunkin believes MTS leadership would have to have been "more polite and loyal."[76] Rosobrnadzor, for its part, is increasingly combative towards any institution that fails to sufficiently conform. In an interview with Roman Lunkin, Dr. Mitskevich shared his belief that the climate of distrust of non-Orthodox fostered by the 2016 Yarovaya "Anti-Terrorist" Law helps explain the troubles faced by his seminary:

> Any law can result in benefit or harm, and unfortunately the Yarovaya Law has brought much harm; it has in essence become an anti-missionary law that has instilled fear among believers and created problems for churches. I am a doctor by profession, and I often think about how not to cause harm but instead to help. Yet the first thought of our security agencies is usually to look for guilt and a concrete reason why someone may be prosecuted. The Church's calling is to spread faith— that is what missionary activity is about. Yet how often are we not healed, helped, or warned here, but forced into a corner straight away, as when Rosobrnadzor suspended the activity of our Moscow Theological Seminary in early 2019.
>
> Our country must try to walk the path of prayer with God and trust for one another, but we are ruled by suspicion, fear, and doubt. There is no desire for reconciliation; everyone is shut away from everyone else behind iron doors. The Yarovaya Law has become a law of intimidation that can be used at any moment against any preacher, whereas there should be an enlightened and respectful attitude towards religious believers.[77]

A number of individuals interviewed by this author in Moscow in May 2019 expressed an opinion similar to one voiced by journalist Dr. William Yoder in March 2020, that MTS "had refused to do the necessary homework and instead chose to accuse the state. No one I heard in Moscow claimed there is a general, state-introduced closing of seminaries in the country. But my impression may be too optimistic."[78] Whatever shortcomings MTS may have been guilty of in terms of paperwork, ongoing troubles with state inspections at a host of additional Protestant institutions would suggest a pattern of discrimination that goes well beyond one seminary's purported insufficient attention to state higher education documentation requirements. This author is in receipt of too many communications from too many beleaguered Russian Protestant educators to believe otherwise.

In the wake of the late February 2020 court decision, Dale Kemp, president of Russian Leadership Ministries, which raises Western financial support for MTS, summarized the seminary's present plight and prospects: "We have no accreditation; we have lost our license in Moscow; we are being pushed out into the churches, offering non-credit seminars." In addition, fire marshal inspections in February-March 2020 generated citations that could cost the equivalent of $50,000 to 60,000 to remedy—in a building to which faculty and students have no access. Still, Kemp noted, there has been no curtailment of MTS instruction underway online, via correspondence, or in its distance learning centers—trends in non-residential education well underway before the school's present troubles.[79] As a last resort, "We are still going to appeal to European courts," even though Russia often ignores their rulings.[80]

The Eurasian Theological Seminary

The Pentecostal Union's Eurasian Theological Seminary (ETS) has faced the same state scrutiny as MTS. Following an inspection 19-22 February 2018, Rosobrnadzor ordered ETS to correct cited violations by 22 March 2018. *Forum* 18's Arnold writes,

> According to the record…on Rosobrnadzor's website, most of these related to how the seminary was run day-to-day, including an apparent lack of consultation with student representatives, lack of provision of sporting and cultural activities, and the absence of particular documents on its website."[81]

Academy of Sciences religion scholar Roman Lunkin concurs with Arnold's assessment: "The misdemeanors of which the Moscow Theological Seminary stands accused are purely bureaucratic."[82]

Dissatisfied with ETS responses, Rosobrnadzor took the seminary to court, leading to a fine of 150,000 rubles ($2,300) by Lyublino District Court on 25 April 2018, which was upheld by Moscow City Court on 2 July 2018. Meanwhile, ETS faced an unplanned Rosobrnadzor inspection 30 April-4 May 2018, which led to a suspension of ETS admissions on 1 June 2018, a suspension of ETS's license on 9 August 2018, and the annulment of its license on 23 November 2018, at which point the seminary was "obliged to stop offering certificated courses."[83]

In contrast to the position taken by Moscow Evangelical Christian Seminary's Sergey Chervonyenko that seminaries are subject to Rosobrnadzor's accreditation as well as licensing standards, Pentecostal Union lawyer Vladimir Ozolin has objected to Rosobrnadzor's

> treating the [Eurasian Theological] Seminary's non-state-accredited theology bachelor's degree as if it corresponded to the degree of theology on the Education Ministry's formal "List of Areas of Higher Education Preparation – Undergraduate." This was despite the materials submitted to the inspection clearly indicating that the [ETS] course was intended for the training of clergy and church personnel and was therefore not subject to the same organizational and administrative requirements as a state-accredited programme.[84]

An official with the Church of God (Cleveland), with which ETS is affiliated, writes that the seminary "did face some extreme inspections on short notice along with just about every other evangelical seminary in Russia." Fortunately for ETS, he writes, on 7 November 2019 the seminary

> received a new license from the Moscow City Department of Education and Science. Again, terminology is different, but we are still in operation. ETS currently gives training to about 850 people, including residential, extension, and online [programs]. It seems that the inspection of the seminaries in 2018 was only the first wave.[85]

As a member of Russia's Public Chamber appointed by Putin in 2006, Bishop Sergei Ryakhovsky, head of Russia's second-largest Pentecostal denomination, is something of a de facto spokesperson for all of Russia's Protestant churches. Nevertheless, he appears to have been powerless to provide effectual cover on behalf of his denomination's ETS. Nor has his appointment by Putin to the Public Chamber impeded increasing numbers of threats to the property of Pentecostal churches in Oryol, Kaluga, Nizhny Novgorod, Novorossiysk, Krasnodar, Tatarstan, and Tula.[86] In the opinion of attorney Ozolin, state restrictions imposed upon Protestant seminaries are part of a more comprehensive effort to exert "pressure…on the non-traditional confessions."[87] The lengthy litigation being endured by MTS & ETS, along with the close state scrutiny of many other Protestant seminaries (and churches), is reminiscent of the concerted court effort over the years to disenfranchise Salvation Army ministry in Russia.[88]

The 2016 Anti-Extremist Law

Forum 18's Victoria Arnold compiled a list of prosecutions in 2018 under the Yarovaya Anti-Extremist Law of 2016. Ostensibly directed at the threat posed by Islamic radicals, it in fact primarily targets Protestants. Of 159 known prosecutions in 2018 under this 2016 law, only 15 took action against Russian Muslims. In contrast, Protestants faced charges of unlawful missionary activity in 104 cases (50 Pentecostals, 39 Baptists, 5 Seventh-day Adventists, and 10 other Protestants).[89] The arbitrariness of Yarovaya Law enforcement is well illustrated by the fate of two churches in 2018 reported by *Forum 18*. The Good News Mission Pentecostal Church in Ufa, Bashkortostan, was fined 30,000 rubles ($4,600) for *failure to display* its official full name at its entrance, whereas an Evangelical Christian-Baptist House of Prayer in the Perm Region was found in violation of the law because it *did display* its full name outside the church. According to the court verdict, the ECB signage amounted to "missionary activity aimed at disseminating information about the beliefs of [the church] among other persons who are not members."[90]

The Moscow Evangelical Christian Seminary

The interdenominational Moscow Evangelical Christian Seminary (MECS) is no stranger to close state oversight. Founded by One Mission

Society, a U.S.-based Evangelical mission agency, MECS was briefly shuttered by Rosobrnadzor in the summer of 2007 for alleged "fire violations and for failing to offer a quality education."[91] MECS recouped and reopened, but it has continued to be the object of Rosobrnadzor inspections, most recently in October 2018. Being one of the last Protestant seminaries to face inspection in 2018, MECS drew lessons from the experience of others. According to MECS administrator Sergey Chervonenko, "Observing the results of the audit at one of the Moscow seminaries, we understood that the process would be difficult and tried to prepare as much as possible." Harold Brown, OMS missionary and MECS board chair, characterized the most recent lead inspector as "tough," but one who in the end upheld the school's accreditation.[92]

Other Protestant Institutions

Representative of Protestant seminary challenges far afield from Moscow is the experience of the Pentecostal Chuvash Bible Centre. In 2007 state authorities shuttered this school on grounds that it "conducted educational activities without authorization" and allegations of fire and sanitation code violations. The school took its grievance to the European Court of Human Rights in 2008 and eventually won its case in 2014.[93]

A Rosobrnadzor inspection of the Evangelical Christian-Baptist North Caucasus Bible Institute (Prokhladny, Kabardino – Balkaria Republic) on 27-28 June 2018 ended with citations for non-compliance with educational, sanitation, and fire safety standards. Prokhladny District Court imposed a fine of 150,000 rubles ($2,300) on 27 August 2018. An additional inspection, 15-19 October 2018, led Rosobrnadzor to charge the institute and Rector Mikhail Chizhma with failure to rectify educational and other violations. In November 2018 Rosobrnadzor suspended the school's right to admit new students. By latest report the institute, nevertheless, continues to offer its educational program to the satisfaction of denominational if not state standards.[94]

Also in November 2018 Kuban Evangelical Christian University (KECS) in Krasnodar had its license temporarily suspended. Originally founded as Lampados Bible College under the sponsorship of the U.S. Christian and Missionary Alliance denomination, this seminary's rector, Gennadi Pshenichny, nevertheless manages a hopeful note: "This past year we faced many challenges as the state education agency paid several visits to our campus. Still, God is faithful and we continue to work and study even though the future may at times seem uncertain."[95]

Further Tightening of State Requirements

Sergey Chervonenko (MECS) anticipates that the next hurdle that Robsobrnadzor may erect is state verification of the degrees held by higher education faculty: "In the future they may well introduce requirements to confirm the level of teaching staff in Russia," an especially ominous prospect for Protestant seminaries.[96] In Russia's current anti-Western climate closer scrutiny of staff degrees does not bode well for these schools which depend heavily upon Western support and whose administrators and faculty so often hold theological degrees from Europe and the U.S. It is widely recognized that Western ties and support taint Protestant institutions and Protestants in general.[97] Case in point is Moscow's Russian-American Christian University (RACU), one of only two Russian Evangelical liberal arts programs to receive state accreditation, along with Zaoksky Adventist University near Tula.[98] RACU's hard-won accreditation, awarded in 2003, was lost in 2009, in good measure because Rosobrnadzor changed accreditation requirements to no longer credit faculty with Western doctorates in calculating the number of qualified instructors.[99]

Russian Protestant seminary faculty are now even beginning to be required to undergo "state-recognized advanced theological training" leading to a "diploma in theological pedagogy" from a secular university, "as absurd as it sounds."[100] Compounding this imposition forced upon Kuban Evangelical Christian University, the secular institute affiliated with Kuban State University that offers this new diploma has already doubled the tuition for this mandatory training.[101]

"Audits" of the Auditors: From Sympathetic to Strongly Critical

On balance, Sergei Chervonenko (MECS) desires to give state auditors the benefit of the doubt:

> After a scheduled inspection of Rosobrnadzor [RON], we reported on the implementation of the requirements and received an unscheduled inspection of RON with a new staff of inspectors. This taught us that different experts can interpret the requirements in different ways; one expert will say "normal," the other – "violation." Yes, that's right, some decisions are subjective. It is necessary to interact with each expert individually. Difficult and unpredictable? Yes. Is it possible to handle this? Definitely possible.... It is important to interact with RON experts; they pay attention to the tone of communication of the tested, the willingness to listen to their comments and involvement in the correction of the shortcomings found. RON experts are living people, no matter how trite it sounds; they value a good attitude (but do not allow attempts to "grease the palm"). And even RON experts can make a mistake. Yes, this is so. They have to study a huge array of documents, and given our religious specificity, the likelihood of error increases.[102]

Even hard-pressed Rector Pshenichny in Kuban can marshal up charity toward individual Rosobrnadzor inspectors:

> When it comes to personal interactions with officials the situation can change.... People begin to ask questions and see the disparity between what they see and hear on TV [about Protestants] and real life. They become much more balanced and open to dialogue. Some of them make efforts to help us. Some become genuinely interested in Christianity.[103]

Nevertheless, Pshenichny judges Rosobrnadzor's overall implementation of oversight as "a profanation of education, relegating it to a piece of paper with a stamp." He openly critiques this state body, which holds a Damocles Sword over the life of his seminary, in a manner that is both searching and courageous. When queried by the author concerning state oversight of private educational institutions, he judged it to be a combination of a) an effort to standardize and ensure quality, b) part of an overall government goal to bring all sectors of Russian society under closer state supervisions, and c) part of state measures to discriminate against, and in some cases, suppress, non-Orthodox faiths:

> It is common knowledge that the overall state of education in Russia leaves much to be desired. Therefore, I would say that it is not at all surprising that the state has taken upon itself the

effort to standardize higher education. However, speaking from my experience in the field of education, I would say that ensuring quality is not a top priority of the Ministry of Education. It is virtually impossible to find people in today's system who would be genuinely interested in education. We hear slogans and goals but that's just words. Most of what we see is a vast gap between what is being proclaimed and even written on paper–and real everyday life. The system is set up in such a way that officials have to give account to their supervisors and so they react only as prompted. The inspections are genuinely interested only in checking off their lists and finding faults with the schools so they can report back to their respective supervisors and prove they are effective. They do not care about education in the least. In this, they are part of the larger system and not necessarily discriminating against one group or another. The tendency is to stifle initiative anywhere and lay [down a] heavy burden, which creates a façade of uniformity and order. This is just how things work.

At the same time the discrimination against non-Orthodox faiths, especially evangelicals, has always been there. It is twofold. First, there are those who are ideologically opposed and purposefully malign and denigrate non-Orthodox believers through every means possible. And then there are those who are "strengthening" the hands of the first group through ignorance. Unfortunately, evangelicals still make up a fraction of the overall population of the country and this works against us because the community at large is still in the dark about who we are. The connection with the West does not help. Current sentiment in the media is anti-West and anti-US.[104]

In the same vein Kursk Protestant educator Aleksandr Spichak writes, "Of course, when it comes to Protestant schools, you cannot escape subjectivity because it is in the air in Russia, when the nationalism and anti-American attitude is promoted everywhere. And there might be men in local administration who would use this opportunity to press more on Protestants."[105] A denominational leader close to the Eurasian Theological Seminary seconds the opinion of Pshenichny and Spichak in reference to dealings with Rosobrnadzor: "To answer your questions, is it a justifiable effort to standardize education? We are not of this opinion. We fulfilled all of the state's demands. But there was no effort from the state to work with us to help us ensure that their standards were met."[106]

Especially telling is Rosobrnadzor's draconian treatment of two secular institutions: the European University of St. Petersburg and the Moscow School of Social and Economic Sciences, private universities with stellar international reputations.[107] Rosobrnadzor cancelled the former's accreditation and revoked its license in 2016 over alleged building code infractions and took possession of most of its campus property in early 2018. Accreditation was restored in July 2018, but not before Rosobrnadzor had dealt the university a near-lethal blow.[108] On 20 June 2019 Rosobrnadzor also revoked the accreditation of the highly regarded Moscow School of Social and Economic Sciences which, however, was restored in March 2020.[109]

Two leading Western professional bodies, the U.S.-based Association for Slavic, East European, and Eurasian Studies (ASEEES) and its sister British Association for Slavic, East European, and Eurasian Studies (BASEEES), publicly addressed their concerns to Russian authorities, expressing "great disappointment" with Rosobrnadzor actions against the two schools. An ASEEES press release described the Moscow School of Social and Economic Sciences as "one of the country's most highly regarded universities" and the European University of St. Petersburg as "another of the country's leading private universities."[110]

Just as bold as Rector Pshenichny's critique of Rosobrnadzor, the European University of St. Petersburg prepared a 24-page "audit" of the auditors entitled "How Does Rosobrnadzor Work: Analysis of Open Data on Supervisory Activities in the Sphere of Higher Education." More accustomed to enumerating the institutional shortcomings of others, Rosobnrnadzor in this instance was subjected to a searching critique of its own ethical and procedural shortcomings. The European University report gave this state higher education watchdog a low, if not failing, grade in a wide-ranging series of findings:

- The number of higher education institutions is decreasing year by year. However, the number of supervisory activities is increasing.

- Private universities are much more likely to be inspected. Effective performance indicators do not significantly reduce the likelihood of an inspection....The actual inspection is largely detached from the monitoring results and it is not always consistent with the performance indicators developed by the Ministry of Education.

- The procedure of selecting experts [auditors] does not prevent the enlisting of specialists who have violated ethical norms in their professional activities. Among these experts there are authors of dissertations with sizeable borrowings from other people's texts. Indicators of the publication activity of such experts demonstrate that they are on average more prone to manipulating formal performance indicators of academic activity than most other lecturers.

- Inspections are increasingly being carried out remotely, in the form of working with documents without visiting the university. The inspectors focus on minor violations mainly related to documenting the work of the institution.[111]

Regarding inspections not conducted on site that are cited in the final bullet, it should be noted that in all known cases Protestant seminaries have undergone in-person inspections. Given their small enrollments, compared to those of most other private institutions and all state universities, might this focused attention on Protestants have more to do with discrimination against a suspect religious minority than with the goal of fostering high educational standards?

Conclusion

In sum, Russian Protestant seminaries are presently undergoing a trial by state inspection that threatens their very existence. Academics Perry Glanzer and Konstantin Petrenko are correct in asserting that the Russian state's "power to license and accredit" is "the power of life and death" over any educational institution.[112]

State justifications for close oversight of Protestant seminaries appear overstated at best and lack credibility at worst. As regards state concerns for quality control, should not the Russian constitution's requirement for separation of church and state take precedence over a secular government's presumption to instruct believers on how best to train their clergy?

Russia's declining student-age population has led leaders in public higher education to lobby the state to curtail private universities and institutes. And on its own account the state has concluded the country needs far fewer tertiary institutions in general. But Russia's Protestant population of approximately two percent means the quite modest enrollments in its non-state-funded seminaries cannot possibly be a demographic threat to public higher education.[113]

The concerted efforts of the administration of President Vladimir Putin to exert ever greater control over all sectors of Russian life is much in keeping with the country's longstanding tradition of authoritarian rule. Russia's Protestant seminaries labor under the additional burden of the common, Russian media-stoked perception of Protestantism as a Western import—and this in a climate of chauvinistic nationalism and xenophobia. A Russian News Agency TASS release of 6 April 2020 underscores this ever-present threat to Protestant seminaries. Proposed Duma legislation would further impair the work of "foreign NGOs," including "foreign-funded educational programmes...likely to be subjected to additional sanction and scrutiny."[114] Such a prospect would further jeopardize those Protestant seminaries that still receive financial support from abroad.

A key question addressed in this study centers on the Russian state's motivation for increased state restrictions on Protestant seminaries. Has it been to ensure quality, or to strengthen state control over all sectors of Russian society, or to discriminate against non-Orthodox believers—or some combination of the three? One Russian Orthodox educator, who prefers not to be identified, rejects the idea that new government requirements placed on Protestant seminaries amounts to persecution. He argues, for example, that Baptists did not do their homework in preparing documents for inspectors. In sum, he sees the government upholding standards for all educational institutions to ensure quality, a process he considers normal and positive.[115]

A contrasting view is held by Dale Kemp of Russian Leadership Ministries who believes the state's desire for improved quality is a minor consideration—if one at all. Rather, he views the goal of increased secular control and discrimination against non-Orthodox to be the chief state motivators, an opinion held by most Protestant educators who have fared poorly in Ministry of Education inspections.[116]

In the present COVID-19 pandemic, Evangelical seminaries and churches, like all other Russian institutions, have closed their doors to gatherings of any size for the duration of the crisis. Acting in bad faith, might Russian authorities prolong restrictions upon gatherings of non-Orthodox beyond the point of medical necessity? Fears that authoritarian regimes might take advantage of emergency measures to undermine the rule of law have already surfaced not only in the case of Russia, but as regards Hungary, Serbia, Azerbaijan, and Kazakhstan.[117]

Finally, a particularly questionable justification for increasing Russian state oversight of private higher education, including Protestant seminaries, is the purported goal of rooting out corruption. Official campaigns against it are a predictable, periodic feature of Russian political life. Unfortunately, a tradition also prevails of a self-aggrandizing bureaucracy seeking its own benefit over the interests of state and society. How then is a corrupt state capable of eliminating corruption in higher education, public or private? And in the case of Protestant seminaries, the Ministry of Education, notwithstanding its proclivity to find fault, does not even bother to charge corruption in Protestant seminaries, where it is rare to non-existent. Similarly, what effort have auditors expended to understand Evangelical subculture when they insist upon letter-of-the-law "No Smoking" signage in a building in which no one smokes?[118]

In contrast to the problematic interventions of Rosobrnadzor, since the 1990s many Protestant theological schools have chosen self-regulation through their own commendably professional Euro-Asian Accrediting Association (E-AAA).[119] The Russian Ministry of Education and Science could learn a great deal from the example of E-AAA in the promotion and facilitation of high professional standards in tertiary education. Dr. Walter Sawatsky (Anabaptist Mennonite Biblical Seminary) details its achievements in a forthcoming publication, "The Amazing Story of E-AAA (Euro-Asian Accrediting Association)." Here we have an enumeration of the association's exemplary role as "a leader in shaping and building up a Slavic Evangelical ministry for the sake of the churches, to foster a consciously Slavic theology, and also contextual sensitivity in Central Asia." In addition to supportive, rather than confrontational, seminary accreditation site visits, E-AAA has facilitated the publication of classroom texts (Bible Pulpit Series), theological serials (especially the bilingual *Bogoslovskie razmyshleniya/Theological Reflections*), Evangelical archival guides and compendia, theological reference works (such as the *Slavic Bible Commentary*),[120] the regular hosting of academic and pedagogical conferences, and especially commendable, the promotion of "cooperation across a spectrum of [theological and national] differences." In contrast, Sawatsky suspects "Putin's new controls on Russian education…had more to do with blocking innovation than seeking 'best practices.'"[121] Thus, it can reasonably be argued that Russian society and the rule of law would best be served if the state simply left its Protestant seminaries to their own devices.

Author's Note:
"Increasing State Restrictions on Russian Protestant Seminaries" was published in Russian translation in *SOVA; Religiya v svetskom obshchestve* on 1 June 2020: https://www.sova-center.ru/religion/publications/2020/06/d42485/; and in *Protestant* on 6 June 2020: protestant.ru/news/analytics/review/article/1558151.

Notes:

1. Mark R. Elliott, retired professor of history, earned a B.A. from Asbury University and an M.A. and Ph.D. from the University of Kentucky. He taught at Asbury University, Wilmore, Kentucky; Wheaton College, Wheaton, Illinois; Samford University, Birmingham, Alabama; and Southern Wesleyan University, Central, South Carolina. At Wheaton College Dr. Elliott served for 13 years as director of the Institute for East-West Christian Studies, and at Samford University he served for six years as director of the Global Center at Beeson Divinity School. He served as editor of the *East-West Church & Ministry Report* (www.eastwestreport.org) from its founding in 1993 through 2017. He now serves as editor emeritus. He is also an Advisory Editor of *Occasional Papers on Religion in Eastern Europe*.

2. "Ivan Smirnov," emails to author, 9 and 12 January 2020.

3. Elizaveta Potapova and Stefan Trines, "Education in the Russian Federation," *World Education News + Reviews*, 6 June 2017; https://wenr.wes.org/2017/06/education-in-the-russian-federation.

4. "Russia: Four Years of Putin's Foreign Agents' Law to Shackle and Silence NGOs," Amnesty International, 18 November 2016; https:www.amnesty.org/en/latest/news/2016/11/russia-four-years-of-putins-foreign-agents-law-to-shackle-and-silence-ngos/.

5. Dmitry A. Suspitsin, "Between the State and the Market: Sources of Sponsorship and Legitimacy in Russian Nonstate Higher Education" in *Private Higher Education in Post-Communist Europe: In Search of Legitimacy*. ed. by Snejana Slantcheva and Daniel C. Levy (London: Macmillan Palgrave, 2017), 157 and 160-61.

6. Decree No. 314, 9 March 2004, "On the System and Structure of Federal Executive Authorities;"https://www.wto.org/english/thewto_e/rus_e/WTACCRUS50_LEG_1.pdf. See also Konstantin Petrenko and Perry L. Glanzer, "The Recent Emergence of Private Christian Colleges and Universities in Russia: Historical Reasons and Contemporary Developments," *Christian Higher Education* 4 (2005), 95.

7. "Putin Signs into Law a Bill on State Accreditation of Religious Schools," *Interfax*, 29 February 2008.

8. No. 273-FZ. See Sergey Chervonenko, "Proverka ot Rosobrnadzora: itogi i mysli [Verification from Rosobrnadzor; Results and Thoughts], 23 August 2019; medium.com@chervonenko/proverka-ot-rosobrnadzora-itogi-i-mysli-b340a766ffc7; Potopova and Trines, "Education," 8; https://www.ilo.org/dyn/natlex/natlex4.detail%3Fp_lang%Den26p_isn%3D93529.

9. Mark Elliott, "New Opportunities, New Demands in the Old Red Empire," *Evangelical Missions Quarterly* 28 (January 1992): 32-39.

10. Mark Elliott, "Protestant Theological Education in the Former Soviet Union," *International Bulletin of Missionary Research* 18 (January 1994): 14.

11. *Spravochnik bogoslovskie uchebnye zavedeniya v stranakh SNG i Baltii* (Moscow: Assotsiatsiya "Dukhovnoe Vozrozhdenie," 1999). See also Hunter Baker, "Russian Seminaries' Enrollment Woes," *Christianity Today Online*, 8 November 2007.

12. https://www.global-regulation.com/translation/russsia/2941574/on-freedom-of-conscience-and-religious-association-act.html.

13. Mark Elliott, "New Restrictive Law on Religion in Russia," *East-West Church & Ministry Report* 5 (Summer 1997): 1-2; Lauren Homer, "Human Rights Lawyer Criticizes New Russian Religion Law," *East-West Church & Ministry Report* 5 (Summer 1997): 2-3; "Commentary on the New Russian Law on Religion," *East-West Church & Ministry Report* 5 (Summer 1997): 3-5; Mark Elliott, "The New Russian Law on Religion: What Is the Fallout for Evangelicals?" *East-West Church & Ministry Report* 5 (Fall 1997): 4-5.

14. Maria Kravchenko, "Inventing Extremists: The Impact of Russian Anti-Extremism Policies on Freedom of Religion or Belief," United States Commission on International Religious Freedom, January 2018; https://www.uscirf.gov/reports-briefs/special-reports/inventing-extremists-the-impact-russian-anti-extremism-policies; Alexei Markevich, "Mission of Russian Christian Education," E. Stanley Jones School of World Missions and Evangelism, Asbury Theological Seminary, 6 May 2019; Anonymous, email to author, 10 February 2020.

15. Katherin Machalek, "Factsheet: Russia's NGO Laws," Freedom House, [2013]; https://freedomhouse.org.

16. Potapova and Trines, "Education;" and Daria Platonova and Dmitry Semyonov, "Russia: The Institutional Landscape of Russian Higher Education" in *25 Years of Transformations of Higher Education Systems in Post-Soviet Countries* (London: Palgrave Macmillan, 2018); link.springer.com/chapter/10.1007/978-3-319-52980-6-13; p. 345.

17. Dmitry A Suspitsin, "Private Higher Education in Russia: The Quest for Legitimacy," Ph.D. dissertation, Pennsylvania State University, 2007; Suspitsyn, "Between the State and the Market," 160-61; Anthony W. Morgan and Nadezhda V. Kulikova, "Reform and Adaptation in Russian Higher Education, An Institutional Perspective," *European Education* 39 (Fall 2007): 42; Potapova and Trines, "Education," 15; and Platonova and Semyonov, "Russia," 345.

18. Morgan and Kulikova, "Reform," 57; and Suspitsyn, "Private Higher Education," 1.

19. Petrenko and Glanzer, "The Recent Emergence," 92.

20. Andrei Kortunov, "Russian Higher Education," *Social Research* 76 (Spring 2009): 215-16. For the Rosobrdnadzor website see obrnadzor.gov.ru/ru/.

21. Potapova and Trines, "Education," 15.

22. "Russia's Higher Education Institutions are Disappearing," khodorkovsky.com/russias-higher-education-institutions-disappearing.

23. "Russia's Higher Education."

24. Potapova and Trines, "Education," 5.

25. "Russia's Higher Education." See also Potapova and Trines, "Education," 4.

26. "Russian Education Minister Calls for Pruning Vast State Higher-Education System," *Chronicle of Higher Education*, 25 July 2008.

27. Gennadi Pshenichny, email to author, 1 November 2019.

28. Aleksandr Spichak, email to author, 11 December 2019.

29. Sergey Chervonenko, email to author, 23 August 2019.

30. John A. Bernbaum, *Opening the Red Door; The Inside Story of Russia's First Christian Liberal Arts University* (Downers Grove, IL: InterVarsity Press, 2019), 190.

31. Olga Zaprometova, email to author, 9 October 2019.

32. Vladimir A. Geroimenko, Grigori A. Kliucharev, and W. John Morgan, "Private Higher Education in Russia: Capacity for Innovation and Investment," *European Journal of Education; Research, Development and Policy* 47 (No. 1, 2012); https://doi.org/10.1111/j.1465-3425.2011.01509.x; Perry L. Glanzer and Konstantin Petrenko, "Private Christian Colleges and Universities in the Former Soviet Union," *East-West Church & Ministry Report* 14 (Spring 2006): 11; and Petrenko and Glanzer, "Recent Emergence," 93.

33. Morgan and Kulikova, "Reform," 55. See also "Russia's Natural Population Decline to Hit 11-Year Record in 2019," *Moscow Times*, 13 December 2019.

34. Potapova and Trines, "Education," 4. See also Kortunov. "Russian Higher Education," 214.

35. Potapova and Trines, "Education," 3. See also Kortunov, "Russian Higher Education," 213.

36. Potapova and Trines, "Education," 2-4. See also Kortunov, "Russian Higher Education," 208.

37. Kortunov, "Russian Higher Education," 208 and 216; Morgan and Kulikova, "Reform," 56.

38. Mark R. Elliott, emails to Russian Protestant educators and leaders, 8 and 29 October 2019; 4 and 8 December 2019; 9 February 2020.

39. Sergey Chervonenko, email to author, 23 August 2019.

40. Anonymous, email to author, 25 October 2019.

41. Roman Lunkin, "Theology for a Select Few: Soviet Déja Vu for Russia's Protestants?" *East-West Church Report* 27 (No. 3, 2019): 11.

42. transparency.org/whatwedo/publication/corruption_perceptions_index_2019. On current state efforts to combat corruption in higher education see "Protivodeistvie korruptsii;" obrnadzor.gov.ru.

43. "The Second Economy of the USSR," *Problems of Communism* 26 (No. 5, 1977): 25-40. Among the subsequent legions of studies of corruption in the Soviet Union see Konstantin M. Simis, *USSR: The Corrupt Society* (New York: Simon and Schuster, 1982); William A. Clark, *Crime and Punishment in Soviet Officialdom; Combatting Corruption in the Political Elite, 1965-1990* (Armonk, NY: M.E. Sharpe, 1993); Louise L. Shelley, *Policing Soviet Society; The Evolution of State Control* (London: Routledge, 1996): and Stephen Lovell, Aleena Ledeneva, and Andrei Rogachevskii, *Bribery and Blat in Russia* (London: Palgrave Macmillan, 2000); James Heinzen, *The Art of the Bribe; Corruption under Stalin, 1943-1953* (New Haven: Yale University Press, 2016).

44. Most stunning and comprehensive is Karen Dawisha, *Putin's Kleptocracy; Who Owns Russia?* (New York: Simon and Schuster, 2014). See also Gilles Favarel-Garrigues, *Policing Economic Crime in Russia; From Soviet Planned Economy to Privatization* (New York: Columbia University Press, 2011); and Vladimir Soloviev, *Empire of Corruption* (Tilburg, Netherlands: Glagoslav Publications, 2012).

45. Morgan and Kulikova, "Reform," 59; Kortunov, "Russian Higher Education," 206.

46. Potapova and Trines, "Education," 3. See also Anna Numtsova, "In Russia, Corruption Plagues the Higher-Education System," *Chronicle of Higher Education* 54 (No. 24, 2008), A18-A20.

47. Nemtsova, "In Russia," A18-A20.

48. Potapova and Trines, "Education," 12-13.

49. Stefan Trines, "Academic Fraud, Corruption, and Implications for Credential Assessment," *World Education News + Reviews,* 10 December 2017; wenr.wes.org/2017/12/academic-fraud-corruption-and-implications-for-credential-assessment.

50. Potapova and Trines, "Education," 13.

51. Olga Khvostunova. "Plagiarism-gate," Institute of Modern Russia, 7 May 2013; imrussia.org/en/nation/453-plagiarism-gate.

52. Olga Zaprometova, email to author, 9 October 2019; Aleksandr Spichak, email to author, 11 December 2019.

53. John Burgess, phone interview with author, 16 September 2019.

54. Perry L. Glanzer and Konstantin Petrenko, "Resurrecting the Russian University's Soul: The Emergence of Eastern Orthodox Universities and Their Distinctive Approaches to Keeping Faith with Tradition," *Christian Scholar's Review* 36 (Spring 2007): 281. See also Petrenko and Glanzer, "Recent Emergence," 90.

55. Glanzer and Petrenko, "Resurrecting," 281.

56. Hunter Baker, "Christian Higher Education Goes to Russia," *Christianity Today Online*, 2 August 2007; Glanzer and Petrenko, "Resurrecting," 273.

57. Lunkin, "Theology," 13.

58. Mikhail Strokan, "Church-State Relations and Property Restitution in Modern Russia," Washington, DC, Center for Strategic & International Relations, 18 August 2016; https://www.csis.org/blogs/post-soviet-post/church-state-relations-and-property-restitution-modern-russia, p. 210. Since the early 1990s the free exercise of religion in post-Soviet space has been a constant theme in the pages of the *East-West Church & Ministry Report* which I served as editor from 1993 through 2017. For a sampling of reporting on state infringements upon the constitutionally protected rights of Russian Protestants see: Victoria Arnold, "RUSSIA: 159 Anti-Missionary Prosecutions in 2018—List," *Forum 18*, 7 May 2019; Victoria Arnold, "RUSSIA: Increasing Land Use Fines 'a Lottery,'" *Forum 18*, 20 March 2018; www.forum18.org/archive.php?article_id=2362; Roman Lunkin, "Do More Than Two Not Gather Together? Interview with Lawyer and Member of Council of Human Rights of the Russian Presidential Administration, Vladimir Ryakhovsky," *Religiya i pravo*, 6 December 2016; http://www2.stetson.edu/~psteeves/relnews/161206a.html; Lauren B. Homer, "Making Sense of the Anti-Missionary Provisions of Russia's Anti-Terrorism Legislation," *East-West Church & Ministry Report* 25 (Spring 2017), 1-7; Roman Lunkin, "Russia: Anti-Evangelism Law Used Against Foreigners Who Speak in Church," *Human Rights Without Frontiers*, 22 September 2016; http://hrwf.eu/russia-anti-evangelism-law-used-against-foreigners-who...; *U.S. Commission on International Religious Freedom, Annual Report 2019*; https://www.uscirf.gov/reports/; U.S. Commission on International Religious Freedom, "Inventing Extremists: The Impact of Russian Anti-Extremism Policies on Freedom of Religion and Belief," 2017; https://www.uscirf.gov/reports-briefs/special-reports/inventing-extremists-the-impact-russian-extremism-policies; U.S. Department of State, *2018 Report on International Religious Freedom: Russia*; https://www.state.gov/reports/2018...: "Yarovaya Law Strikes Protestants; Interview with Historian of Religion Elena Glavatska," *Ploitsovet*, 19 January 2018; https://www2.stetson.

edu/~psteeves/relnews/180119c.html; William Yoder, "A Commentary on Russia's New Anti-Terror Legislation" 15 July 2016; rea-moskva.org.

59. Lunkin, "Theology," 13. See also Sophia Kishkovsky, "Russia to Return Church Property," *New York Times*, 23 November 2010.

60. Lunkin, "Theology," 13.

61. Lunkin, "Theology," 11.

62. Victoria Arnold, "RUSSIA: Obstructions to Protestant Theological Education 'Systemic, Intentional'?" *Forum 18*, 25 March 2019.

63. Arnold, "RUSSIA: Obstructions."

64. https://www.global-regulation.com/translation/russia/2941574/on-freedom-of-conscience-and-religious-associations-act.html.

65. Chervonenko, "Proverka."

66. Kortunov, "Russian Higher Education," 204.

67. Potapova and Trines, "Education," 17; Lunkin, "Theology," 11.

68. Chervonenko, "Proverka."

69. Arnold, "RUSSIA: Obstructions."

70. Kortunov, "Russian Higher Education," 204.

71. Elliott, "Protestant Theological Education," 14; Dale Kemp, email to author, 25 February 2020; russianleadership.org/our-ministry/. A goal for 2020 for Russian Leadership Ministries is to facilitate the opening of additional distance learning centers in Smolensk, Bryansk, Elabuga, and Krasnodar. *Moscow Theological Seminary Annual Report, 2019.*

72. Arnold, "RUSSIA: Obstructions;" Dale Kemp, email to author, 25 February 2020.

73. "Court Revokes License of Moscow Theological Seminary of Evangelical Christians-Baptists," Invictory.org, 28 February 2020; translated in *Russia Religion News*; https://www2.stetson.edu/~psteeves/relnews/200228a.html; Peter Mitskevich, "Words from the President – December 2019," 28 December 2019; https://baptist.org.ru/en/news/view/articles/1535153. See also Lunkin, "Theology," 11-12; Michael Thom, "Russia Shuts Down Baptist and Pentecostal Seminaries," 2 April 2019; https://Baptist.org.ru/en/news/vies/article/153515; https://www.chvnradio.com/christian-news/russia-shuts-down-baptist-and-pentecostal-seminaries. Markevich related to MTS professor Nikolai Kornilov that documentation required by state inspectors was amounting to a mountain of paperwork. Nikolai Kornilov, interview, 23 May 2019.

74. William Yoder, "Peter Mitskevich, New President of the Russian Union of Evangelical Christians-Baptists," *China Christian Daily*, 12 June 2018; Roman Lunkin, interview, 22 May 2019.

75. Lunkin, "Theology," 12.

76. Roman Lunkin, interview, 22 May 2019.

77. Lunkin, "Theology," 14. See also Peter Mitskevich, "Words from the President-February 2020," 14 February 2020; https://baptist. org.ru/en/news/view/article/1539124.

78. William Yoder, email to author, 14 March 2020.

79. Over the past decade non-traditional instruction, especially online, has been a growing trend worldwide, now accelerating in the midst of the present corona virus pandemic [winter-spring 2020]. A recent survey of Evangelical seminaries worldwide documents the post-Soviet region of Eastern Europe and Central Asia as a leader in the movement. Paul Clark, "Survey on Online Theological Education," Overseas Council, 2019, 4.

80. Dale Kemp phone interview, 30 March 2020.

81. Arnold, "RUSSIA: Obstructions."

82. Lunkin, "Theology," 11.

83. Arnold, "RUSSIA: Obstructions."

84. Arnold, "RUSSIA: Obstructions."

85. Church of God, emails to author, 4 and 31 December 2019.

86. Church of God, emails to author, 4 and 31 December 2019; Lunkin, "Theology," 13-14.

87. Arnold, "RUSSIA: Obstruction."

88. Ian Traynor, "Russian Court Lifts Salvation Army Ban," *The Guardian*, 6 March 2002.

89. Arnold, "RUSSIA: 159." See also Yoder, "A Commentary;" "Yarovaya Law;" Kate Shellnutt, "Russian Evangelicals Penalized Most Under Anti-Evangelism Law," *Christianity Today*, 7 May 2019; and U.S. Department of State, *2018 Report on International Religious Freedom: Russia*; https//www.state.gov/reports/2018-report-on-international-religious-freedom/russia/.

90. Arnold, "RUSSIA: 159." See also U.S. Department of State, *2018 Report*, 7.

91. Baker, "Russian Seminaries' Enrollment Woes."

92. Brown explained that Alexander Tsutserov (St. Andrews University Ph.D.) is president of Moscow Evangelical Christian Seminary (MECS), while Sergey Chervonenko (Asbury Theological Seminary D.Min.) is president of Evangelical Christian Seminary at the same location. Brown phone interview, 22 November 2019, and Brown email, 25 February 2020. Chervonenko explained the same arrangement to the author in a 21 May 2019 interview in Moscow.

93. "Biblical Centre of the Chuvash Republic v Russia: ECHR, 12 June 2014;" https://swarb.co.uk/biblical-centre-of-the-chuvash-republic-v-russia-echr-12-jun-2014; Arnold, "RUSSIA: Obstructions."

94. Arnold, "RUSSIA: Obstructions;" Lunkin, "Theology," 12.

95. Gennadi Pshenichny, email to author, 1 November 2019. See also "Rosobrnadzor Bans Acceptance of Students to Seminary of Evangelical-Lutheran Church," *Interfax*, 13 December 2019; interfax- religion.com/?act=news&div=15405.

96. Sergey Chervonenko, "Proverka."

97. Gennadi Pshenichny, email to author, 1 November 2019; John Burgess, phone interview with author, 16 September 2019; Church of God, emails to author, 4 and 31 December 2019; Scott Cunningham, phone interview, 31 March 2020; Dale Kemp, phone interview, 30 March 2020; Gennadi Sergienko, interview, 24 May 2019; U.S. Department of State, *2018 Report*, 16.

98. Mikhail Kulakov, *God's Soviet Miracles: How Adventists Built the First Protestant Seminary in Russian History* (Nampa, ID: Pacific Press Publishing Association, 1993); Petrenko and Glanzer, "The Recent Emergence," 90-91.

99. Bernbaum, *Opening the Red Door*, 199; Mark R. Elliott, "Review of *Opening the Red Door; The Inside Story of Russia's First Christian Liberal Arts University* in *Christianity Today Online*, 17 February 2020.

100. Gennadi Pshenichny, email to author, 1 November 2019.

101. Gennadi Pshenichny, email to author, 1 November 2019; Harold Brown, phone interview, 22 November 2019. In a 24 May 2019 interview Dr. Gennadi Sergienko also attested to Rosobrnadzor's move toward state validation of theological faculty.

102. Sergey Chervonenko, "Proverka."

103. Gennadi Pshenichny, email to author, 1 November 2019.

104. Gennadi Pshenichny, email to author, 1 November 2019.

105. Aleksandr Spichak, email to author, 11 December 2019.

106. Church of God, email to author, 4 December 2019.

107. Potapova and Trines, "Education," 17-18; "Russia's Higher Education."

108. "Russia Certifies European University at St. Petersburg's Master's Programs," *Moscow Times*, 5 July 2019.

109. "Rector Zuev's Comments Regarding the Denial of Accreditation for Activities in the Field of Higher Education," December 2019; https://www.msses.ru/en/about/news/4083/; Grigory Yudin, "Overzealous Regulators Are Closing in on Russian Universities," *Moscow Times*, 10 July 2018; "MSSES Got Accreditation Back," linkedin.com/school/shaninka.

110. "ASEEES Statement Concerning the Moscow School of Social and Economic Sciences (Shaninka)," 20 July 2018; https://www.aseees.org/advocacy/aseees-statement-concerning-moscow-school-social-and-economic-sciences-shaninka. See also *Scholars at Risk Network*, 20 June 2018; https://www.scholarsatrisk.org/report/2018-06-20-moscow-school-of-social-and-economic-sciences/.

111. Katerina Guba, Aleksandra Makeeva, Mikhail Sokolov, and Anzhelika Tsivinskaya, "Kak rabotaet Rosobrnadzor: analiz otkrytykh dannykh o kontrol'no—nadzornoi deyatel'nost v sfere vysshego obrazovaniya ["How Does Rosobrnadzor Work: Analysis of Open Data on Supervisory Activities in the Sphere of Higher Education]," St. Petersburg: European University in St. Petersburg, 2017; https//eusp.org/en/news/how-does-rosobrnadzor-work-analysis-of-open-data-supervisory-activities-in-the-sphere-of-higher-education.

112. Glanzer and Petrenko, "Private Christian Colleges," 11.

113. The two percent estimate is based on the current Russian Federation population of 145,872,000 (*United Nations World Population Review*; worldpopulationreview.com) and Roman Lunkin's calculation that the number of the country's Protestant adherents "is approaching 3 million" (Pyat'sot let vmeste," *Nezavisamaya gazeta—Religii*, 18 October 2017; http://www.ng.ru/ng_religii/2017-10-18/13_430_together.html).

114. William Yoder, "Russian Seminaries Remain in Limbo: The Future Remains Uncertain," 6 April 2020.

115. Russian Orthodox educator interview, 23 May 2019.

116. Dale Kemp, phone interview, 30 March 2020.

117. Radio Free Europe/Radio Liberty releases: "EU Warns Against Using Pandemic to Undermine Democracy" and "Members of U.S. Congress Criticize Additional Powers for Orban in Corona Emergency," 31 March 2020; "Podcast: COVID-19 and the 'Dictatorship of Law,'" 6 April 2020; "Amnesty Slams 'Offensive' Against Human Rights in Eastern Europe, Central Asia," 12 April 2020; "HRW Says Azerbaijan Abuses COVID-19 Restrictions to Crack Down on Critics," 16 April 2020; and "Rights Defenders Accuse Kazakh Authorities of Using Coronavirus Restrictions to Stifle Dissent," 20 April 2020.

118. Gennadi Sergienko, interview, 24 May 2019.

119. www.e-aaa.org.

120. Peter Penner, "Review of The Slavic Bible Commentary," *East-West Church & Ministry Report* 25 (Winter 2017): 4-5.

121. Walter Sawatsky would like to see "more voices urging the Russian Education department to back off of its efforts to control theological schools." Walter Sawatsky, email to author, 1 April 2020.

Appendix: Interviews and Correspondence

Interviews

John Burgess (phone), Pittsburgh Theological Seminary, 16 September 2019
Harold Brown (phone), One Mission Society, 22 November 2019
Sergey Chervonenko, Moscow Evangelical Christian Seminary, 21 May 2019
Scott Cunningham (phone), Overseas Council, 31 March 2020
Dale Kemp (phone), Russian Leadership Ministries, 30 March 2020
Nikolai Kornilov, Moscow Theological Seminary, 23 May 2019
Roman Lunkin, Russian Academy of Sciences, 22 May 2019
Russian Orthodox educator, 23 May 2019
Gennadi Sergienko, Second Evangelical Christian-Baptist Church and Moscow Theological Seminary, 24 May 2019

Email Correspondence

Sergey Chervonenko, Moscow Evangelical Christian Seminary, 23 August 2019
Church of God (Cleveland) official, 4 and 31 December 2019
Gennadi Pshenichny, Kuban Evangelical Christian University, 1 November 2019
Russian denominational leader, 25 October 2019
Walter Sawatsky, Anabaptist Mennonite Biblical Seminary, 14 March 2020
"Ivan Smirnov," 9 and 12 January 2020
Aleksandr Spichak, Trinity Video Seminary, 11 December 2019
William Yoder, Russian Evangelical Alliance, 14 March 2020
Olga Zaprometova, St. Filaret Orthodox Christian Institute, 9 October 2019

www.ingramcontent.com/pod-product-compliance
Lightning Source LLC
Chambersburg PA
CBHW071458040426
42444CB00008B/1394